TERMS OF EMPOWERMENT

Salvation Army Women in Ministry

**Female Ministry: or, Woman's Right to
Preach the Gospel**
First published 1859, London.
Reprinted 1891, Salvation Army Printing & Publishing Offices,
London.
Reprinted 1975, The Salvation Army
Supplies Printing and Publishing
Department, New York.
Reprinted 2001, The Salvation Army, USA Eastern Territory,
440 West Nyack Road, West Nyack, NY 10994

Woman
First published 1930, Fleming H. Revell Company, New York.
Reprinted 2001, The USA Eastern Territory.

Keeping the Dream Alive
© 2001, The USA Eastern Territory.
Cover art by Erich Asperschlager

ISBN: 0-89216-101-9

❦ FOREWORD ❦

On the cusp of century 21, CNN produced a popular series, "The Next Millennium," to which it invited Bishop Stephen Charleston to contribute a statement on the "Future of Faith." The bishop, a native American and a distinguished Episcopal educator and church leader, identified the acceptance and empowerment of women as full and equal partners in the life of the churches as a clear sign of what is to come. He is far from alone in recognizing that the turning point marked by the widening acceptance of the ordination of women to ministry toward the end of the 20th century was a major breakthrough presaging an unprecedented role for women in the church of this new millennium. Catherine Booth was far in advance of her time in recognizing the ministry potential of women and in rigorously defending the biblical legitimacy of public ministry for called and gifted women to proclaim a Gospel of oneness in Christ—a oneness that transcends all distinctions of ethnicity, social status, or gender (Galatians 3:28).

Catherine's bold exegesis was needed then and is needed now. Thankfully, an ever more impressive body of scholarly literature is at the disposal of today's women; it clarifies scriptures skewed for centuries to exclude women from public ministry and spiritual leadership. The Army Mother flung open a door to ministry through which a great company of courageous women have moved into lifetimes of productive service to the cause of Christ and global mission. The Army was not alone in affording such opportunities to women, for the holiness movement in America, among other movements, provided a platform for generations of eloquent preachers of righteousness—women whose anointing and ordination by the Spirit could not be denied by those who heard them. But no part of the Church has so consistently encouraged the public ministry of women, both married and single, as has The Salvation Army. Their right to respond to God's call and to assume whatever ministry tasks or leadership roles for which they were equipped was written into the foundation documents of the movement.

Evangeline Booth, herself a charismatic leader of uncommon achievement, sensed the emerging potential of women and the promise of their part in the burgeoning economic life of American society in the early decades of the 20th century. Still, she knew that Christian women—Army women—needed a call to arms, a liberating manifesto of God-ordained possibility, a ringing emancipation proclamation, if they were to rise to the challenges that now lay before them. Her lecture entitled simply, "Woman," is a most remarkable document given the times, and is, in its way, as farsighted and prophetic a statement as that of the Army Mother. These documents, one from the heart of the 19th century and the next from the early 20th century, are different in style and emphasis but resonate with that same liberating Gospel call for women to claim fully that freedom for which "Christ has set us free" (Galatians 5:1 and 3:28).

It is appropriate in the dawning of this new millennium that a contemporary call to claim the full promise of this hard-won heritage should be sounded. Commissioner Kay F. Rader (R) D.D., former world president of Women's Organizations for The Salvation Army, was asked to do so. A tireless advocate for women around the world, she has sought to encourage and empower them toward their full potential in public ministry and leadership. Tenaciously, she has insisted on full and equal consideration of their gifting and calling, whether they are married or single. Kay Rader speaks out of a passionate commitment to mission and an urgent awareness that playing our part in reaching our world for Christ must require the fullest possible deployment of the whole of the Christian force, and not its male contingent alone. She clearly identifies those biases and subtly prejudicial procedures and practices that have deactivated and demotivated women who have the call of God upon them. Recalling Catherine Booth's own grave fears that women of the Army in future generations might fail to rise to the opportunities that had been afforded them, she summons today's women to "keep in step with the Spirit" (Galatians 5:25), for "where the Spirit of the Lord is, there is freedom" (2 Corinthians 2:17).

Secular feminism has sensitized our generation to the kinds of customs and mores that, often unintentionally, demean and victimize women. But secular feminists have too often based an abrasive rhetoric on false assumptions and in the process alienated much of the Christian community, driving them into a defensive and reactionary posture. In the din and dust of battle, the sane and liberating message of the Gospel for women has sometimes been lost. And the example of the Lord Jesus, who so often "companioned women to dignity" has been forgotten. An almost paranoid backlash against a radical feminism that threatens to erode the foundations of family and the institution of marriage, already under attack, has caused some churches to deny women their historic right to make "full proof of their ministry." In this context, while other denominations are still embroiled in endless debate, The Salvation Army is, and must continue to be, a standard bearer of Gospel promise for all women, continuing to accord them the respect and acceptance our founders sought to guarantee, affording ever-expanding opportunities for women to enrich the life of the Church and enhance its effectiveness. This is an issue that impacts the whole church and its mission. Men, as well as women, need to hear the voices that speak through these pages. They speak compellingly of keeping Catherine Booth's dream alive. This volume is commended to both women and men who believe in that dream and care about the cause of Christ, the mission of the Army, and the liberating purpose of God. 🍎

General Paul A. Rader (R)
President of Asbury College
Wilmore, Kentucky

❧ Table of Contents ❧

Catherine Mumford Booth

Catherine Mumford Booth

Born on Jan. 17, 1829, to John and Sarah Mumford, Catherine Mumford became a committed Christian at an early age. In 1852 she met William Booth, a Methodist minister with whom she soon found she had strong agreement on the Church's role in social ministry. They were married three years later.

Catherine was a fervent believer in women's right to preach the gospel, and her husband urged her to share her views. The result was the pamphlet "Female Ministry," published in 1859. Though Catherine was reluctant to preach herself, William encouraged her. In a Whitsunday service in Gateshead in 1860, Catherine felt the Holy Spirit come upon her and rose to the podium. William turned to the congregation and said, "My dear wife wants to say a word." By the time she finished speaking, many in the audience were weeping audibly. William impulsively announced that she would preach the evening service. It was the beginning of a long and fruitful pulpit ministry.

In 1865, William and Catherine founded the Christian Mission in London's East End, a ministry that by 1878 would be known as The Salvation Army. Catherine worked tirelessly, campaigning against social injustice, including deplorable working conditions for women. She and William had eight children, all of whom grew up to be Salvation Army officers. In a day when women with children were expected to remain at home, Catherine continued her career as preacher, evangelist, social worker, and author. Her writings on holiness and the sacraments formed the foundations of Salvation Army theology. At her death in 1890, she left a legacy of care and faith that would make her world-famous as co-founder of The Salvation Army and "the Army mother."

❧ Female Ministry ❧
By Catherine Booth

The first and most common objection urged against the public exercises of women is that they are unnatural and unfeminine. Many labour under a very great but common mistake, that of confounding nature with custom. Use, or custom, makes things appear natural, which, in reality, are very unnatural; while, on the other hand, novelty and rarity make very natural things appear strange and contrary to nature. So universally has this power of custom been felt and admitted, that it has given birth to the proverb, "Use is second nature."

Making allowance for the novelty of the thing, we cannot discover anything either unnatural or immodest in a Christian woman, becomingly attired, appearing on a platform or in a pulpit. By *nature* she seems fitted to grace either. God has given to woman a graceful form and attitude, winning manners, persuasive speech, and, above all, a finely-toned emotional nature, all of which appear to us eminent *natural* qualifications for public speaking. We admit that want of mental culture, the trammels of custom, the force of prejudice, and one-sided interpretations of Scripture, have hitherto almost excluded her from this sphere; but before such a sphere is pronounced to be unnatural, it must be proved either that woman has not the *ability* to teach or to preach, or that the possession and exercise of this ability unnaturalises her in other respects; that so soon as she presumes to step on the platform or into the pulpit she loses the delicacy and grace of the female character. Whereas, we have numerous instances of her retaining all that is most esteemed in her sex, and faithfully discharging the duties peculiar to her own sphere, and at the same time taking her place with many of our most useful speakers and writers.

Why should woman be confined exclusively to the kitchen and the distaff, any more than man to the field and workshop? Did not God, and has not nature, assigned to man *his* sphere of labour, "to till the ground and to dress it?" And, if exemption is claimed from this kind of toil for a portion of the male sex, on the ground of their possessing ability for intellectual and moral pursuits, we must be allowed to claim the same privilege for women; nor can we see the exception allowed to claim the same privilege for women; nor can we see the exception more *unnatural* in the one case than in the other, or why God in this solitary instance has endowed a being with powers which He never intended her to employ.

Unnecessary Fear

There seems to be a great deal of unnecessary fear of woman occupying any position which involves publicity, lest she should be rendered unfeminine by the indulgence of ambition or vanity; but why should woman any more than man be charged with ambition when impelled to use her talents for the good of her race? Moreover, as a labourer in the *Gospel* her position is much higher than in any other public capacity; she is at once shielded from all coarse and unrefined influences and associations her very vocation tending to exalt and refine all the tenderest and most womanly instincts of her nature. As a matter of fact it is well known to those who have had opportunities of observing the private character and deportment of women engaged in preaching the Gospel, that they have been amongst the most amiable, self-sacrificing, and unobtrusive of their sex.

"We well know," says the late Mr. Gurney, a minister of the Society of Friends, "that there are no women among us more generally distinguished for modesty, gentleness, order, and right submission to their brethren, than those who have been called by their Divine Master into the exercise of the Christian ministry."

Who would dare to charge the sainted Madame Guyon, Lady Maxwell, the talented mother of the Wesleys, Mrs. Elizabeth Fry, Mrs. Smith, Mrs. Whiteman, or Miss Marsh with being unwomanly or ambitious. Some of these ladies we know have adorned by their private virtues the highest ranks of society, and won alike from friends and enemies, the highest eulogies as to the devotedness, purity, and sweetness of their lives. Yet these were all more or less public women, every one of them expounding and exhorting from the Scriptures to mixed companies of men and women. Ambitious doubtless they were; but theirs was an ambition akin to His, who for the "joy that was set before Him, endured the cross, despising the shame:" and to his, who counted all things but dung and dross, and was willing to be regarded as the off-scouring of all things that he might win souls to Jesus and bring glory to God. Would that the Lord's people had more of this ambition.

According to the Bible

Well, but, say our objecting friends, how is it that those whose names you mention, and many others, should venture to preach when female ministry is *forbidden in the Word of God?* This is by far the most serious objection which we have to consider—and if capable of substantiation, should receive our immediate and cheerful acquiescence; but we think that we shall be able to show, by a fair and consistent interpretation, that the very opposite view is the truth; that not only is the public ministry of woman unforbidden, but absolutely enjoined by both precept and example in the Word of God.

First, we will select the most prominent and explicit passages of the New Testament referring to the subject, beginning with I Corinthians 11:4,5: *"Every man praying or prophesying, having his head covered, dishonoureth his head. But every woman that prayeth or prophesieth with her head uncovered, dishonoureth her head; for that is all one as if she were shaven,"* etc. "The character," says one talented writer, "of the prophesying here referred to by the Apostle is defined in I Corinthians 14:3, 4, and 31st verses. The reader will see that it was directed to the edification, exhortation, and comfort of believers; and the result anticipated was the conviction of unbelievers and unlearned persons. Such were the public services of women which the Apostle allowed, and such was the ministry of females predicted by the prophet Joel, and described as a leading feature of the Gospel dispensation. Women who speak in assemblies for worship under the influence of the Holy Spirit, assume thereby no personal authority over others; they simply deliver the messages of the Gospel, which imply obedience, subjection, and responsibility, rather than authority and power."

Dr. A. Clarke, on this verse, says, "Whatever may be the meaning of praying and prophesying in respect to the man, they have precisely the same meaning in

4

respect to the woman! So that some women at least, as well as some men, might speak to others to edification, exhortation, and comfort. And this kind of prophesying or teaching was predicted by Joel 2:28, and referred to by Peter (Acts 2:17). And had there not been such gifts bestowed on woman, the prophecy could not have had its fulfillment. The only difference marked by the Apostle was that the man had his head uncovered, because he was representative of Christ; the woman had hers covered because she was placed by the order of God in subjection to the man; and because it was the custom both among Greeks and Romans, and among the Jews an express *law* that no woman should be seen abroad without a veil. This was and is the custom through all the East, and none but public prostitutes go without veils; if a woman should appear in public without a veil, she would *dishonour her head—her husband.* And she must appear like those women who have their hair shaven off as the punishment of adultery."

We think that the view above given is the only fair and common-sense interpretation of this passage. If Paul does not here recognize the *fact* that women did actually pray and prophesy in the primitive Churches, his language has no meaning at all; and if he does not recognize their *right* to do so by dictating the proprieties of their appearance while so engaged, we leave to objectors the task of educating any sense whatever from his language. If, according to the logic of Dr. Barnes, the Apostle here, in arguing against an improper and indecorous mode of performance, forbids the performance itself, the prohibition extends to the *men* as well as to the women; for Paul as expressly reprehends a man praying with *his* head covered, as he does a woman with *hers* uncovered. With as much force might the Doctor assert that in reproving the same Church for their improper celebration for the Lord's Supper (I Corinthians 11:20,21), Paul prohibits all Christians, in every age, celebrating it at all.

"The question with the Corinthians was not whether or not the woman should pray or prophesy at all; that question had been settled on the day of Pentecost; but whether, as a matter of convenience, they might do so without their veils." The Apostle kindly and clearly explains that by the law of nature and of society it would be improper to uncover her head while engaged in acts of public worship. We think that the reflections cast on these women by Dr. Barnes and other commentators are quite gratuitous and uncalled for. Here is no intimation that they ever had uncovered their heads while so engaged; the fairest presumption is that they had not, nor ever would till they knew the Apostle's mind on the subject. We have precisely the same evidence that the men prayed and preached with their hats on, as that women removed their veils, and wore their hair dishevelled, which is simply none at all. We cannot but regard it as a signal evidence of the power of prejudice, that a man of Dr. Barnes's general clearness and acumen should condescend to treat this passage in the manner he does.

The Doctor evidently feels the untenableness of his position; and endeavours, by muddling two passages of distinct and different bearing, to annihilate the argument fairly deducible from the first. We would like to ask the Doctor on what authority he makes such an exception as the following; "But this cannot be interpreted as meaning that it is improper for females to speak or pray in meetings of their own sex." Indeed but according to the most reliable statistics we possess, two-thirds of the whole Church is, and always has been, composed of their own sex. If, then, "no rule of the New Testament is more positive than this, viz., that women are to keep *silence* in the Churches," on whose authority does the Doctor license them to speak to by far the larger portion of the Church?

A lawyer writing to us on the above passage, says, "Paul here takes for granted that women were in the habit of praying and prophesying; he expresses no surprise nor utters a syllable of censure; he was only anxious that they should not provoke unnecessary obloquy by laying aside their customary headdress or departing from the dress which was an indicative of modesty in the country in which they lived. This passage seems to prove beyond the possibility of dispute that in the early times women were permitted to speak to the 'edification and comfort' of Christians, and that the Lord graciously endowed them with grace and gifts for this service. What he did then, may He not be doing now?"

"It seems truly astonishing that Bible students, with the second chapter of the Acts before them, should not see that an imperative decree has gone forth from God, the execution of which women cannot escape; whether they like or not, they *'shall'* prophesy throughout the whole course of this dispensation; and they have been doing so, though they and their blessed labours are not much noticed."

Well, but say our objecting friends, hear what Paul says in another place:—*"Let your women keep silence in the churches, for it is not permitted unto them to speak; but they are commanded to be under obedi-*

ence, as also saith the law. And if they will learn* any-thing, let them ask their husbands at home; for it is a shame for women to speak in the Church" (I Corinthians 14:34,35). Now let it be borne in mind this is the same Apostle, writing to the same Church, as in the above instance. Will any one maintain that Paul here refers to the same kind of speaking as before? If so, we insist on his supplying us with some rule of interpretation which will harmonize this unparalleled contradiction and absurdity.

Taking the simple and common-sense view of the two passages, viz., that one refers to the devotional and religious exercises in the Church, and the other to inconvenient asking of questions, and imprudent or ignorant talking, there is no contradiction or discrepancy, no straining or twisting of either. If, on the other hand, we assume that the Apostle refers in both instances to the same thing, we make him in one page give the most explicit directions how a thing shall be performed, which in a page or two further on, and writing to the *same* Church, he expressly forbids being performed at all. We admit that *"it is a shame for women to speak in the Church,"* in the sense here intended by the Apostle; but before the argument based on these words can be deemed of any worth, objectors must prove that the "speaking" here is synonymous with that concerning the manner of which the Apostle legislates

---

* *"Learning* anything by asking their husbands," cannot mean *preaching,* which is not learning, but *teaching* the way of God. It cannot mean being inspired by the Holy Ghost to foretell future events. No woman, having, either taught or prophesied, would have to ask her husband at home at home before she knew what she had done, or understood what she had said. Such women would be only fit to "learn in silence with all subjection." The reference is evidently to subjects *under debate.*

8

in I Corinthians 11. Dr. A. Clarke, on this passage, says, "According to the prediction of Joel, the Spirit of God was to be poured out on the women as well as the men, that they might prophesy, that is, *teach.*" And that *they* did prophesy or teach is evident from what the Apostle says (I Corinthians 11), where he lays down rules to regulate this part of their conduct while ministering in the Church. All that the Apostle opposes here is their *questioning, finding fault, disputing, etc.,* in the Christian Church, as the Jewish men were permitted to do so in their synagogues (see Luke 2:46); together with attempts to usurp authority over men by setting up their judgment in opposition to them; for the Apostle has reference to acts of disobedience and arrogance, of which no woman would be guilty who was under the influence of the Spirit of God.

Explanation of Words

The Rev. J. H. Robinson, writing on this passage, remarks: "The silence imposed here must be explained by the verb, to speak (λαλεῖυ), used afterwards. Whatever that verb means in this verse, I admit and believe the women were forbidden to do *in the Church*. But what does it mean? It is used nearly three hundred times in the New Testament, and scarcely any verb is used with so great a variety of adjuncts.

In *Schleusner's Lexicon,* its meaning is traced under *seventeen* distinct heads, and he occupies two full pages of the book in explaining it. Among other meanings he gives *"respondeo, rationem redo, præcipio, jubeo;* I answer, I return a reason, I give rule or precept, I order, decree."

In *Robinson's Lexicon* (Bloomfield's edition), two

pages nearly are occupied with the explanation of this word; and he gives instances of its meaning, "as modified by the text, where the sense lies, not so much in (λαλεῖν) (lalein) as in the adjuncts." The passage under consideration is one of those to which he refers as being so "modified by the context."

Greenfield gives, with others, the following meanings of the word: "to prattle—*be loquacious as a child; to speak in answer—to answer,* as in John 19:10; *harangue, plead,* Acts 9:29; 21. *To direct, command,* Acts 3:22."

In *Liddel and Scott's* Lexicon, the following meanings are given: "*to chatter, babble;* of birds, *to twitter, chirp;* strictly, *to make an inarticulate sound,* opposed to articulate speech: but also generally *to talk, say.*"

It is clear then that (λαλεῖν) may mean something different from mere speaking, and that to use this word in a prohibition does not imply that absolute silence or abstinence from speaking is enjoined, but, on the contrary, that the prohibition applies to an *improper kind of speaking* which is to be understood, not from the word itself, but, as Mr. Robinson says, from 'the context.' Now, 'the context' shows that it was not *silence* which was imposed upon women in the Church, but only a refraining from such speaking as was inconsistent with the words, 'they are commanded to be under obedience,' or, more literally, 'to be obedient:' that is, they were to refrain from such questionings, dogmatic assertions, and disputations, which would bring them into collision with the men, ruffle their tempers, and occasion an unamiable volubility of speech. This kind of speaking, and this alone, as it appears to me, was forbidden by the Apostle in the passage before us. This kind of speaking was the only supposable antagonist to, and violation of, 'obedience.' Absolute silence was not essential to that 'obedience.'

My studies in "Bible Criticism," etc., have not informed me that a woman must cease to speak before she can obey; and I am therefore led to the irresistible conclusion that it is not *all* speaking in the Church which the Apostle forbids, and which he pronounces to be shameful; but, on the contrary, a pertinacious, inquisitive, domineering, dogmatical kind of speaking, which, while it is unbecoming in a *man,* is shameful and odious in a *woman,* and especially when that woman is in the Church, and is speaking on the deep things of religion.

Parkhurst in his lexicon, tells us that the Greek word 'lalein,' which our translation renders speak, is *not* the word used in Greek to signify "to speak with premeditation and prudence," but is the word used to signify "to speak imprudently and without consideration, and is that applied to one who lets his tongue run but does not speak to the purpose, but says nothing." Now unless Parkinson is utterly wrong in his Greek, which it is apprehended no one will venture to affirm, Paul's fulmination is not launched against speech with premeditation and prudence, but against speech devoid of these qualities. It would be well if all speakers of the male as well as the female sex were obedient to this rule.

We think that with the light cast on our text (I Corinthians 14:34,35), by eminent Greek scholars above quoted, there can be no doubt in any unprejudiced mind as to the true meaning of the verb "to speak" in this connection. And we find from Church history that the primitive Christians thus understood it, for that women did actually speak and preach amongst them we have indisputable proof.

Not Confined Only to Men

God had promised in the last days to pour out His Spirit upon all flesh, and that the *daughters,* as well as the sons of mankind, should prophesy. And Peter says most emphatically, respecting the outpouring of the Spirit on the day of Pentecost, *"This is that which is spoken of by the prophet Joel,"* etc. (Acts 2:16–18). Words more explicit, and an application of prophecy more direct than this, does not occur within the range of the New Testament.

Commentators say, "If women have the gift of prophecy, they must not use that gift in public." But God says, by His prophet Joel, they *shall* use it, just in the same sense as the sons use it. When the dictation of men so flatly opposes the express declaration of the "sure word of prophecy," we make no apology for its utter and indignant rejection.

The Early Church Fathers were slow to accept the fact that among the primitive Christians preaching was not confined to men, but that God had, according to His promise, on the day of Pentecost poured out His Holy Spirit upon believers—men and women, old and young—that they should *prophesy,* and they *did* so. The prophesying spoken of was not the foretelling of events, but the *preaching* to the world at large the glad tidings of salvation by Jesus Christ. For this purpose it pleased God to make use of *women* as well as men.

"It is plainly the duty of every Christian to insist upon the fulfillment of the will of God, and the abrogation of every single thing inconsistent therewith. I would draw attention to the fact that Phoebe, a Christian woman whom we find in our version of the Scripture (Romans 16:1) spoken of only as any common

12

servant attached to a congregation, was nothing less than one of those gifted by the Holy Spirit *for publishing the glad tidings,* or *preaching the Gospel.* The manner in which the Apostle (whose only care was the propagation of evangelical truth) speaks of her, shows that she was what he in Greek styled her, a deacon or preacher of the Word. Other translators speak of *her* (because she was a *woman*) only as 'a *servant* of the Church which is at Cenchrea.' The men 'deacons' they styled ministers, but a woman on the same level as themselves would be an anomaly, and therefore she was to be only the *servant* of men *ministers,* who constituted *the Church!"*

The Apostle says of her—*"I commend unto you Phoebe our sister, who is a minister (deacon) of the Church which is at Cenchrea: that ye receive her in the Lord, as becometh saints, and that ye assist her in whatever business she hath need of you."* To the common sense of disinterested minds it will be evident that the Apostle could not have requested more for any one of the most zealous of men preachers than he did for Phoebe! They were to assist her *"in whatever business"* she might require their aid. Hence we discern that she had no such trifling position in the primitive Church as at the present time Episcopal dignitaries attach to deacons and deaconesses! Observe, the same Greek word is used to designate her that was applied to all the Apostles and to Jesus Himself. For example: *"Now I say that Jesus Christ was a minister (deacon) of the circumcision"* (Romans 15:8). *"Who then is Paul, and who is Apollos, but ministers by whom ye believed"* (I Corinthians 3:5). *"Our sufficiency is of God; who also hath made us able ministers of the new testament"* (II Corinthians

3:6). *"In all things approving ourselves as the minis-ters of God"* (6:4). The idea of a woman deacon in the *"three orders!"*—It was intolerable; therefore, let her be a "servant." Theodoret however says, "The fame of Phoebe was spoken of throughout the world. She was known not only to the Greeks and Romans, but also to the Barbarians," which implies that she had travelled much and propagated the Gospel in foreign countries.

"Salute Andronicus and Junia, my kinsmen and my fellow-prisoners, who are of note among the Apostles; who also were in Christ before me" (Romans 21:7). By the word "kinsmen" one would take Junia to have been a man; but Chrysostom and Theophylact, who were both Greeks, and consequently knew their mother tongue better than our translators, say *Junia was a woman.* "Kinsmen" should therefore have been ren-dered "kinsfolk"; but with our translators it was out of all character to have a *woman* of note amongst the Apostles, and a fellow-prisoner with Paul for the Gospel: therefore let them be kinsmen!

Justin Martyr, who lived till about A.D. 150, says, in his dialogue with Trypho, the Jew, that "both men and women were seen among them who had the extraordi-nary gifts of the Spirit of God, according as the prophet Joel had foretold, by which he endeavoured to convince the Jews that the latter days were come."

Dodwell, in his dissertations of Irenæus says, "that the gift of the spirit of prophecy was given to others besides the Apostles: and that not only in first and sec-ond, but in the third century—even to the time of Constantine—all sorts and ranks of men had these gifts; yea, and *women* too."

Eusebius speaks of Potomania Ammias, a prophetess,

in Philadelphia, and others, "who were equally distin-guished for their love and zeal in the cause of Christ."

"The scriptural idea," says Mrs. Phoebe Palmer,[1] "of the terms preach and prophesy, stands so inseparably connected as one and the same thing, that we should find it difficult to get aside from the fact that women did preach, or, in other words, prophesy, in the early ages of Christianity, and have continued to do so down to the present time to just the degree that the spirit of the Christian dispensation had been recognized. And it is also a significant fact, that to the degree denomination, who have once favoured the practice, lose the freshness of their zeal, and as a consequence, their primitive sim-plicity, and, as ancient Israel, yield to a desire to be like surrounding communities, in a corresponding ratio are the labours of females discountenanced."

The Scripture in Context

If any one still insists on a literal application of this text, we beg to ask how he disposes, of the preceding part of the chapter where it occurs. Surely, if one verse be so authoritative and binding, the whole chapter is equally so; and therefore, those who insist on a literal applica-tion of the words of Paul, under all circumstances and through all time, will be careful to observe the Apostle's order of worship in their own congregations.

But, we ask, where is the minister who lets his whole Church prophesy one by one, and he himself sits still and listens while they are speaking, so that all things may be done decently and in order? But Paul as express-

---

[1] Mrs. Palmer was to give her home on East 15th Street to The Salvation Army, which was to become the Army's first general hospital in the United States, forerunner to the Booth Medical Center, Flushing, N.Y.

ly lays down this order as he does the rule for women, and he adds, *"The things that I write unto you are the commandments of the Lord"* (ver. 37). Why then do not ministers abide by these directions? We anticipate their reply—"Because these directions were given to the Corinthians as temporary arrangements; and, though they were the commandments of the Lord to them at that time, they do not apply to all Christians in all times." Indeed; but unfortunately for their argument, the prohibition of women speaking even if it meant what they wish, was given amongst those very directions, and to the Corinthians *only:* for it reads, *"Let your women keep silence,"* etc.; and for aught this passage teaches to the contrary, Christian women of all other Churches might do what these women were forbidden to do; until, therefore, they must excuse us declining to do so of the 24th verse; and we challenge them to show any breach of the Divine law in one case more than the other.

Another passage frequently cited as prohibiting female labour in the Church, is I Timothy 2:12,13. Though we have never met with the slightest proof that this text has any reference to the public exercises of women; nevertheless, as it is often quoted, we will give it a fair and thorough examination. "It is primarily an injunction," says the Rev. J.H. Robinson, "respecting her personal behaviour at home. It stands in connection with precepts respecting her apparel and her domestic position; especially her relation to her husband. No one will suppose that the Apostle forbids a woman to 'teach' absolutely and universally. Even objectors would allow her to teach her own sex in private; they would let her teach her servants and children, and, perhaps, her husband too. If he were ignorant of the Saviour, might she

16

not teach him the way to Christ? If she were acquainted with languages, arts, or sciences, which he did not know, might she not teach him these things? Certainly she might! The 'teaching,' therefore which is forbidden by the Apostle, is not every kind of teaching any more than, in the previous instance, his prohibition of speaking applied to every kind of speaking in the Church; but it is such teaching as is domineering, and as involves the usurpation of authority over the man. This is the only teaching forbidden by St. Paul in the passage under consideration.

"If this passage be not a prohibition of every kind of teaching, we can only ascertain what kind of teaching is forbidden by the modifying expressions with which *didaskein* stands associated: and for anything these modifying expressions affirm to the contrary, her teaching may be public, reiterated, urgent, and may comprehend a variety of subjects, provided it be not dictatorial, domineering, nor vociferous; for the, and then only, would it be incompatible with her obedience."

The Rev. Dr. Taft says, "This passage should be rendered 'I suffer not a woman to teach *by* usurping authority over the man.' This rendering removes all the difficulties and contradictions involved in the ordinary reading, and evidently gives the meaning of the Apostle." [Editorial paraphrase: Rev. Dr. Taft goes on to indicate that if you accept the idea of a just and equal society where men and women are equally concerned and responsible, you cannot believe that Paul is denying the right of women to teach and pray.]

"It will be found," says another writer, "by an examination of this text with its connections, that the teaching here alluded to stands in necessary connection with usurping authority, as though the Apostle had said, the

Gospel does not alter the relation of women in view of priority, for Adam was first formed, then Eve.

"This prohibition," says the before–mentioned lawyer, "refers exclusively to the private life and domestic character of woman, and simply means that an ignorant or unruly woman is not to force her opinions on the man whether he will or no. It has no reference whatever to good women living in obedience to God and their husbands, or to women sent out to preach the Gospel by the call of the Holy Spirit."

If the context is allowed to fix the meaning of *didaskein* in this text, as it would be in any other, there can be no doubt in any honest mind that the above is the only consistent interpretation; and if it be, then this prohibition has no bearing whatever on the religious exercises of women led and taught by the Spirit of God: and we cannot forbear asking on whose skirts the mischief resulting from the false application of this text will be found?

Thank God the day is dawning with respect to this subject. Women are studying and investigating for themselves. They are claiming to be recognized as responsible beings, answerable to God for their convictions of duty; and, urged by the Divine Spirit they are overstepping those unscriptural barriers which the Church has so long reared against its performance.

Whether the Church will allow women to speak in *her* assemblies can only be a question of time; common sense, public opinion, and the blessed results of female agency will force her to give us an honest and impartial rendering of the solitary text on which she grounds her prohibitions. Then, when the true light shines and God's works take the place of man's traditions, the doctor of divinity who shall teach that Paul commands woman to be silent when God's Spirit urges her to speak, will be regarded much the same as we should regard an astronomer who should teach that the sun is the earth's satellite.

Beyond the Accepted Role

Another argument urged against female preaching is, that it is unnecessary; that there is plenty of scope for her efforts in private, in visiting the sick and poor and working for the temporalities of the Church. Doubtless woman ought to be thankful for any sphere for benefiting her race and glorifying God. But we cannot be blind to the supreme selfishness of making her so welcome to the hidden toil and self-sacrifice, the hewing of wood and the drawing of water, the watching and waiting, the reproach and persecution attaching to her Master's service, without allowing her the honour which He has attached to the ministration of His Gospel. Here, again, man's theory and God's order are at variance. God says, *"Them that honour me I will honour."* Our Lord links the joy with the suffering, the glory with the shame, the exultation with the humiliation, the crown with the cross, the finding of life with the losing of it. Nor did He manifest any such horror at female publicity in His cause, as many of His professed followers appear to entertain in these days. We have no intimation of His reproving the Samaritan woman for her public proclamation of Him to her countrymen; nor of His rebuking the women who followed Him amidst a taunting mob on his way to the cross. And yet, surely, *privacy* was *their* proper sphere. On one occasion He *did* say, with reference to a woman, *"Verily, I say unto you, wheresoever this Gospel shall be preached in the whole world, there shall also this, that this woman hath done, be told for a memorial of her"* (Matthew 26: 13; see also Luke 7:37-50).

As to the obligation devolving on woman to labour for her Master, I presume there will be no controversy. The particular sphere in which each individual shall do this must be dictated by the teachings of the Holy Spirit and the gifts with which God has endowed her. If she have the necessary gifts, and feels herself called by the Spirit to preach, there is not a single word in the whole book of God to restrain her, but many, very many, to urge and encourage her. God says she SHALL do so, and Paul prescribed the manner in which she shall do it, and Phoebe, Junia, Philip's four daughters, and many other women, actually did preach and speak in the primitive Churches. If this had not been the case, there would have been less freedom under the new than under the old dispensation, a greater paucity of gifts and agencies under the Spirit than under the law, fewer labourers when more work to be done. Instead of the destruction of caste and division between the priesthood and the people, and the setting up of a spiritual kingdom in which all true believers were "kings and priests unto God," the division would have been more stringent and the disabilities of the common people greater. Whereas we are told again and again in effect, that in *"Christ Jesus there is neither bond nor free, male nor female, but ye are all one in Christ Jesus."*

The Record of Scripture

We commend a few passages bearing on the ministrations of women under the old dispensation to the careful consideration of our readers. *"And Deborah, a prophetess, the wife of Lapidoth, she judged Israel at that time,"* etc. (Judges 4:4–10). There are two particulars in this passage worthy of note. First, the authority of Deborah as a prophetess, or revealer of God's will to Israel, was acknowledged and submitted to as implicitly as in the cases of the male judges who succeeded her. Secondly, she is made the military head of ten thousand men, Barak refusing to go to battle without her.

Again, in II Kings 12:12–20, we have an account of the king sending the high-priest, the scribe, etc., to Huldah, the prophetess, the wife of Shallum, who dwelt at Jerusalem, in the college, to enquire at her mouth the will of God in reference to the book of the law which had been found in the House of the Lord. The authority and dignity of Huldah's message to the king does not betray anything of that trembling diffidence or abject servility which some persons seem to think should characterize the religious exercises of woman. She answers him as the prophetess of the Lord, having the signet of the King of kings attached to her utterances.

"The Lord gave the word, and great was the company of those that published it" (Psalm 68:11). In the original Hebrew it is, "Great was the company of women publishers, or women evangelists." Grotius explains this passage, "The Lord shall give the word . . . so that he would call those which follow the great army of preaching women, victories, or female conquerors." How comes it that the feminine word is actually excluded in this text? That it is there as plainly as any other word no Hebrew scholar will deny. It is too much to assume that as our translators could not *alter* it, as they did "Diaconon" when applied to Phoebe, they preferred to leave it out altogether rather than give a prophecy so unpalatable to their prejudice. But the Lord gives the

word, and He will choose whom He pleases to publish it, not withstanding the condemnation of translators and divines.

"For I brought thee up out of the land of Egypt, and redeemed thee out of the house of servants; and I sent before thee Moses, Aaron, and Miriam" (Micah 6:4).

God here classes Miriam with Moses and Aaron, and declares that *He* sent her before His people. We fear that had some of our friends been men of Israel at that time, they would have disputed such a leadership.

In the light of such passages such as these, who will dare to dispute the fact that God did, under the old dispensation, endow His handmaidens with the gifts and calling of prophets answering to our present idea of preachers. We are thankful to find abundant evidence that the *"spirit of prophecy which is the testimony of Jesus,"* was poured out on the female as fully as on the male disciple, and "His daughters and His handmaidens" prophesied. We commend the following texts from the New Testament to the careful consideration of our readers.

"And she (Anna) was a widow of about fourscore and four years, which departed not from the temple, but served God with fastings and prayers night and day. And she coming in at that instant, gave thanks likewise unto the Lord, and "spake of Him to all them that looked for redemption in Jerusalem" (Luke 2:37, 38). Can any one explain wherein this exercise of Anna's differed from that of Simeon, recorded just before? It was in the same public place, the temple. It was during the same service. It was equally public, for she *"spake of Him to all who looked for redemption in Jerusalem."*

Jesus said to the two Marys, *"All hail! And they came and held Him by the feet, and worshiped Him. Then*

*said Jesus unto them, Be not afraid: go, tell my
brethren that they go before me into Galilee"* (Matthew
28:9,10). There are two or three points in this beautiful
narrative to which we wish to call the attention of our
readers.

First, it was the *first* announcement of the glorious
news to a lost world and a company of forsaking disciples. *Second,* it was as *public* as the nature of the case
demanded; and intended ultimately to be published to
the ends of the earth.

Third, Mary was expressly commissioned to reveal
the fact to the Apostles; and thus she literally became
their teacher on that memorable occasion. Oh, glorious
privilege, to be allowed to herald the glad tidings of a
Saviour risen! How could it be that our Lord chose a
woman to this honour? Well, one reason might be that
the male disciples were all missing at the time. They all
forsook Him and fled. But woman was there, as she had
ever been, ready to minister to her risen, as to her dying,
Lord—

> *"Not she with traitorous lips her Saviour stung;*
>
> *Not she denied Him with unholy tongue;*
>
> *She, whilst Apostles shrunk could danger brave;*
>
> *Last at the cross, and earliest at the grave."*

But surely, if the dignity of our Lord or His message were
likely to be imperiled by committing this sacred trust to
a woman, He who has guarded by legions of angels
could have commanded another messenger; but, as if
intent on doing her honour and rewarding her unwa-
vering fidelity, he reveals Himself *first* to her; and, as an
evidence that He had taken out of the way the curse
under which she had so long groaned, nailing it to His

cross, He makes her who had been first in the transgression, first also in the glorious knowledge of complete redemption.

Refer to Acts 1:14, and 2:1,4. We are in the first of these passages expressly told that the women were assembled with the disciples on the day of Pentecost; and in the second, that the cloven tongues sat upon them *each,* and the Holy Ghost filled them *all,* and they spake as the Spirit gave them utterance. It is beside the point to argue that the gift of tongues was a miraculous gift, seeing that the Spirit was the primary bestowment. The tongues were only emblematical of the office which the Spirit was henceforth to sustain to his people. The Spirit was given alike to the female as to the male disciple, and this is cited by Peter (16,18), as a peculiar speciality of the latter dispensation. What a remarkable device of the Devil that he has so long succeeded in hiding this characteristic of the latter day glory! *He* knows, whether the Church does or not, how eminently detrimental to the interests of his kingdom have been the religious labours of woman; and while her Seed has mortally bruised his head, he ceases not to bruise her heel; but the time of her deliverance draweth nigh.

"Philip the Evangelist had four daughters, virgins, which did prophesy" (Acts 11:9). From Eusebius, the ancient ecclesiastical historian, we learn that Philip's daughters lived to a good old age, always abounding in the work of the Lord. "Mighty luminaries," he writes, "have fallen asleep in Asia. Philip, and two of his virgin daughters, sleep at Hierapolis; the other, and the beloved disciple, John, rest at Ephesus."

"And I entreat thee also, true yokefellow, help those women which laboured with me in the Gospel, with

Clement also, and with other my fellow-labourers" (Philippians 4: 3).

This is a recognition of *female labourers,* not *concerning* the Gospel but *in* the Gospel, whom Paul classes with Clement, and other of his fellow-labourers. Precisely the same terms applied to Timotheus, whom Paul styles a *"minister of God, and his fellow-labourer in the Gospel of Christ"* (I Thessalonians 3:2).

Again, *"Greet Priscilla and Aquila, my helpers in Christ Jesus; who have for my life laid down their own necks; unto whom not only I give thanks, but all the Churches of the Gentiles"* (Romans 16:3,4).

The word translated helpers means fellow-labourers, associates, coadjutors, workers together, assistants, joint labourers, colleagues. In the New Testament the world helpers is used to refer only to co-workers, helpers in a Christian work, or Christian teachers. How can these terms, with any show of consistency, be made to apply merely to the exercise of hospitality towards the Apostle, or the duty of private visitation? To be a partner, coadjutor, or joint worker with a preacher of the Gospel, must be something more than to be His waiting-maid.

Again, *"Salute Tryphena and Tryphosa, who labour in the Lord. Salute the beloved Persis, which laboured much in the Lord"* (Romans 16:12). Dr. Clarke, on this verse, says, "Many have spent much useless labour in endeavouring to prove that these women did not preach. That there were prophetesses as well as prophets in the Church we learn, and that a woman might pray or prophesy provided that she had her head covered we know; and, according to St. Paul (I Corinthians 14: 3), whoever prophesied spoke unto others to edification, exhortation, and comfort, and, that no preacher can do more, every person must acknowledge. Because, to edify, exhort, and comfort, are the prime ends of the Gospel ministry. If women thus prophesied, then women preached."

"There is neither Jew nor Greek, there is neither male nor female, for ye are all one in Christ Jesus" (Galatians 3:28). If this passage does not teach that in the privileges, duties, and responsibilities of Christ's Kingdom, all differences of nation, caste, and sex are abolished, we should like to know what it does teach, and wherefore it was written. (See also I Corinthians 7:22).

As we have before observed, the text, I Corinthians 14:34,35, is the *only one* in the whole Book of God which even by a false translation can be made prohibitory of female speaking in the church; how comes it then, that by this one isolated passage, which, according to our best Greek authorities, is wrongly rendered and wrongly applied, woman's lips have been sealed for centuries, and the *"testimony of Jesus, which is the spirit of prophecy,"* silenced, when bestowed on her? How is it that this solitary text has been allowed to stand unexamined and unexplained? Surely there must have been some unfaithfulness, "craftiness," and *"handling of the Word of Life deceitfully"* somewhere. Surely the love of caste and unscriptural jealousy for a separated priesthood has had something to do with this anomaly. By this course divines and commentators have involved themselves in all sorts of inconsistencies and contradictions; and worse, they have nullified some of the most precious promises of God's Word. They have set the most explicit predictions of prophecy at variance with apostolic injunctions, and the most immediate and wonderful operations of the Holy Ghost in direct opposition "to positive, explicit, and universal rules."

Constrained by the Holy Ghost

Notwithstanding, however, all this opposition to female ministry on the part of those deemed authorities in the Church, there have been some in all ages in whom the Holy Ghost has wrought so mightily, that at the sacrifice of reputation and all things most dear, they have been compelled to come out as witness for Jesus and ambassadors of His Gospel. As a rule, these women have been amongst the most devoted and self-denying of the Lord's people, giving indisputable evidence by the purity and beauty of their lives, that they were led by the Spirit of God. Now, if the Word of God forbids female ministry, we would ask how it happens that so many of the most devoted handmaidens of the Lord have felt themselves constrained by the Holy Ghost to exercise it? Surely there must be some mistake somewhere, for the Word and the Spirit cannot contradict each other. Either the Word does not condemn women preaching, or these confessedly holy women have been deceived. Will anyone venture to assert that such women as Mrs. Elizabeth Fry, Mrs. Fletcher of Madeley, have been deceived with respect to their call to deliver the Gospel messages to their fellow-creatures? If not, then God does not call and qualify women to preach, and His Word, rightly understood, cannot forbid what His Spirit enjoins.

Further, it is a significant fact, which we commend to the consideration of all thoughtful Christians, that the public ministry of women has been eminently owned of God in the salvation of souls and the edification of his people. Paul refers to the *fruits* of his labours as evidence of his Divine commission (I Corinthians 9:2). *"If I am not an Apostle unto others, yet doubtless I am to you: for the seal of mine Apostleship are ye in the Lord."* If this criterion be allowed to settle the question respecting a woman's call to preach, we have no fear as to the result. A few examples of the blessing which has attended the ministrations of females, may help to throw some light on this matter of a Divine call.

At a missionary meeting held at Columbia, March 26th, 1824, the name of Mrs. Smith, of the Cape of Good Hope, was brought before the meeting, when Sir Richard Otley, the chairman, said, "The name of Mrs. Smith has been justly celebrated by the religious world and in the colony of the Cape of Good Hope. I heard a talented missionary state that wherever he went in that colony, at 600 or 1,000 miles from the principal seat of government, among the natives of Africa, and wherever he saw persons converted to Christianity, the name of Mrs. Smith was hailed as the person from whom they received their religious impressions; and although no less than ten missionaries, all men of piety and industry, were stationed in that settlement, the exertions of Mrs. Smith alone were more efficacious, and had been attended with greater success, than the labours of those missionaries combined." The Rev. J. Campbell, missionary to Africa, says, "So extensive were the good effects of her pious exhortations, that on my first visit to the colony, wherever I met with persons of evangelical piety, I generally found that their first impressions of religion were ascribed to Mrs. Smith."

Mrs. Mary Taft, the talented lady of the Rev. Dr. Taft, was another eminently successful labourer in the Lord's vineyard. "If," says Mrs. Palmer, "the criterion by which we may judge of a Divine call to proclaim salvation be by the proportion of fruit gathered, then to the commission of Mrs. Taft is appended the Divine signature, to a degree pre-eminently unmistakable. In reviewing her diary, we are constrained to believe that not one minister in five hundred could produce so many seals to their ministry. An eminent minister informed us that of those who had been brought to Christ through her labours, over two hundred entered the ministry. She seldom opened her mouth in public assemblies, either in prayer or speaking, but the Holy Spirit accompanied her words in such a wonderful manner, that sinners were convicted, and, as in apostolic times, were constrained to cry out, 'What must we do to be saved?' She laboured under the sanction and was hailed as a fellow-helper in the Gospel by the Revs. Messrs. Mather, Pawson, Hearnshaw, Blaborne, Marsden, Bramwell, Vasey, and many other equally distinguished ministers of her time.

The Rev. Mr. Pawson, when President of the Wesleyan Conference, writes as follows to a circuit where Mrs. Taft was stationed with her husband, where she met with some gainsayers:—"It is well known that religion has been for some time at a very low ebb in Dover. I therefore could not help thinking that it was a kind providence that Mrs. Taft was stationed among you, and that, by the blessing of God, she might be the instrument of reviving the work of God among you. I seriously believe Mrs. Taft to be a deeply pious, prudent, modest woman. I believe the Lord hath owned and blessed her labours very much, and many, yea, very many souls have been brought to the saving knowledge of God by her preaching. Many have come to hear her out of curiosity, who would not have come to hear a man, and have been awakened and converted to

God. I do assure you there is much fruit of her labours in many parts of our connection."

Mrs. Fletcher, the wife of the sainted vicar of Madely, was another of the daughters of the Lord, on whom was poured the spirit of prophecy. This eminently devoted lady opened an orphan house, and devoted her time, her heart, and her fortune, to the work of the Lord. The Rev. Mr. Hodson, in referring to her public labours, says, "Mrs. Fletcher was not only luminous but truly eloquent—her discourses displayed much good sense, and were fraught with the riches of the Gospel. She excelled in the poetry of an orator which can alone supply the place of all the rest, that eloquence which goes directly to the heart. She was the honoured instrument of doing much good; and the fruit of her labours is now manifest in the lives and tempers of numbers who will be her crown of rejoicing in the day of the Lord." The Rev. Henry Moore sums up a fine eulogium on her character and labours by saying, "May not every pious churchman say, Would to God all the Lord's people were such prophets and prophetesses!"

Miss Elizabeth Hurrell travelled through many counties in England, preaching the unsearchable riches of Christ; and very many were, through her instrumentality, brought to a knowledge of the truth, not a few of whom were afterwards called to fill very honourable stations in the Church.

From the Methodist Conference, held at Manchester, 1787, Mrs. Wesley wrote to Miss Sarah Mallett, whose labours, while very acceptable to the people, had been opposed by some of the preachers:—"We give the right hand of fellowship to Sarah Mallett, and have no objection to her being *a preacher in our connection,* so long as she preaches Methodist doctrine, and attends to our discipline."

The Right to Teach

We have endeavoured in the foregoing pages to establish, what we sincerely believe, that woman has a *right* to teach. Here the whole question hinges. If she has the *right,* she has it independently of any man-made restrictions, which do not equally refer to the opposite sex. If she has the right, and possesses the necessary qualifications, we maintain that, where the law of expediency does not prevent, she is at liberty to exercise it without any further pretensions to inspiration than those put forth by the male sex. If, on the other hand, it can be proved that she has not the right, but that imperative silence is imposed upon her by the Word of God, we cannot see who has authority to relax or make exceptions to the law.

If commentators had dealt with the Bible, on other subjects as they have dealt with it on this, taking isolated passages, separated from their explanatory connections, and insisting on a literal interpretation of the words of our version, what errors and contradictions would have been forced upon the acceptance of the Church, and what terrible results would have accrued to the world. On this principle the Universalist will have all men unconditionally saved, because the Bible says "Christ is the Saviour of all men," etc. The Antinomian, according to this rule of interpretation, has most unquestionable foundation for his dead faith and hollow profession, seeing that St. Paul declares over and over again that men are saved by faith and not by works. The Unitarian, also, in support of that soul-withering doctrine, triumphantly refers to numerous passages which, taken alone, teach only the humanity of Jesus. In short, "there is no end to the errors in faith and practice which have resulted from taking isolated passages, wrested from their proper connections, or the light thrown upon them by other Scriptures, and applying them to sustain a favourite theory." Judging from the blessed results which have almost invariably followed the ministrations of women in the cause of Christ, we fear it will be found, in the great day of account, that a mistaken and unjustifiable application of the passage, *"Let your women keep silence in the Churches,"* has resulted in more loss to the Church, evil to the world, and dishonour to God, than any of the errors we have already referred to.

And feeling, as we have long felt, that this is a subject of vast importance to the interests of Christ's kingdom and the glory of God, we would most earnestly commend its consideration to those who have influence in the Churches. We think it a matter worthy of their consideration whether God intended woman to bury her talents and influence as she now does? And whether the circumscribed sphere of woman's religious labours may not have something to do with the comparative non-success of the Gospel in these latter days.

Evangeline Cory Booth

Evangeline Cory Booth

Eva Booth was born on Christmas Day in 1865, the seventh of eight children born to William and Catherine Booth. At five years of age, she preached her first "sermon" at her family's kitchen table to a congregation of dolls.

Deferring to her father's wishes, Eva never married. "I am not sure that if you married you would be given every opportunity to use your many talents for the Lord," William told Eva when she asked his permission to wed another officer. William told others close to him, "I have other plans for Eva." But Eva did want to be a mother, so she adopted and raised four children and served as spiritual mother to countless others.

Eva rose rapidly in the ranks of The Salvation Army, leading her first congregation at age 21 in Marylebone, England. Despite the opposition of violent mobs and the hostility of local magistrates, she worked feverishly to convert sinners to Christ. Seeming to thrive under oppression, she won antagonists over through the force of her personality and the sincerity of her faith. She was appointed commander of the Army in Canada in 1896 and commander of the Army in the United States in 1904, when she began to use the name Evangeline. In 1934, she was elected to serve as the Army's fourth General.

Evangeline Booth was a forceful and flamboyant speaker, often appearing in costume and seasoning her sermons with music or drama. Though she had her detractors as well as her admirers, no one ever questioned her genuine compassion and devotion to saving the lost. She was "promoted to Glory" in New York State in 1950, 11 years after her retirement as General.

❦ Woman ❦

By Evangeline Booth

During those wonderful years of progress and pageantry which brought the nineteenth century to a close, there lived and laboured a great Irishman whose name will never be forgotten in the East. He was a man of immense ability and supreme integrity who devoted his entire career to the honest administration of the Imperial Customs of China. After forty years of absence from Europe, he returned at last to London, and he was asked what changes in that great metropolis impressed him most. His answer aroused no little interest. "The women," said he, simply, "are now going to business."

It was the emergence of womanhood that took Sir Robert Hart by surprise—the girls who hurried to the city in the morning by train and street-car and subway, and, having earned a livelihood, hurried out of the city at night. Yet that was the situation, not in the New York, the Chicago, the San Francisco of this year of grace, 1930, but in the slow-moving, old-fashioned, conservative England—the prewar England of twenty-five years ago. Even at that date, and in that county, the women had begun to go to business.

To the keen eye of Sir Robert Hart, accustomed to scenes of human life in East and West, here was a change that pervaded all other changes, a revolution that embraced all other revolutions. The automobile may plough a highway through the pathless desert; but the new era of womanhood is more than locomotion. The airplane may fly from pole to pole; but here is more than aviation. Bridges may leap over the deepest chasms and the broadest rivers, tunnels may pierce the most formidable mountains, small rivulets may have become vast reservoirs refreshing the city, and calling forth a myriad growths along its banks; but here is more than engineering. Mighty edifices, exceeding the Tower of Babel in altitude, may mingle their pinnacles with the clouds; but here is more than the magic of the builder. The flickering candle may have been superseded by the electric lamp; but here is more than illumination. The electric telegraph with its crude taps, the telephone with its sounds, the wireless with its mystery, may have welded the world into one vast whispering gallery; but here is more than acoustics. The camera may record the artless gestures of the infant and the fleeting colours of the sunset; but here is more than photography. To an omniscience, penetrating as the eye of God Himself, our bodies may be as transparent as glass; but here is more than the X-ray. Mass production may pour forth commodities in an incalculable profusion; but here is more than commerce. For the change that has come to women is a change, not in environment merely, not in wealth and habits merely, not in occupation merely, but in the very mind, the very being of the race itself.

As a woman, standing in the front lines of service to humanity, it is with an unbounded enthusiasm of gratitude that I hail the dawn of this long-awaited day of opportunity. The forces of prejudice, of selfishness, of ignorance, which have arrested the progress and curtailed the influence of womankind for centuries, are receding from the foreground of the future, and with astonished vision we look upon the limitless fields of progress. Across all oceans, however tempestuous, over all frontiers, however mountainous, into all countries, however remote and inhospitable, the women's movement is spreading, the exhilaration and invigoration of its spirit is in the very air we breathe, bracing the nerves, stimulating the will, and reinforcing the faculties.

Sometimes we are told that the girl of the West is abandoning the sound standards of modesty and self-respect. She has dismissed her chaperone. She has boy friends for her companions. She wears clothes which allow an unimpeded athleticism to her limbs. She cuts her skirt an inch above, instead of an inch below the knee. She shows her arms in the subway.

But in some, at least, of these matters, has she had any choice? How could she go to business like a man and retain her chaperone? Never has youth tolerated the idea of being out of the fashion, and I do not believe that this eager, vivacious, good-humoured daughter of democracy has had any unworthy motive in her costumes and activities. That some girls fall victims to moral perils is, alas, too true. But when has it not been the truth? On the whole, the girl of today is well able to take care of herself, and makes an excellent wife and mother.

Nor is it only in the West that girls, with life pulsating in their veins, are gathered into schools and colleges, there to develop their powers, spiritual, mental and physical, for the more abundant life, which they were created to live. In Asia and Africa, the path of progress by education, by hygiene, by healing has been cleared of obstacles and, every year, that path is thronged with an increasing company of pilgrims whose eager faces are turned towards the dawn of a new day. There is no country in the world where women, however ill-used, however illiterate, are not beginning, at least, to think about the long overdue chance of going to business.

In China, a lady of fashion no longer thinks that she is required by social caste and traditional custom to bind her feet, lest she be suspected of walking, and sheathe her finger-nails in shields of gold and silver, lest she be accused of doing housework. In Japan, there is no longer a law permitting parents and guardians to compel a girl to play the part of a geisha, and legally, she is free. In India, the Parliament at Delhi has passed legislation which prohibits child-marriage, with its humiliating aftermath of lifelong widowhood; slowly but surely, the custom known as purdah (or seclusion of women in the Zenana) is breaking down; Western medicine is relieving women's pain, and the closed lattice is gradually opening to let in the light and fresh air which alone can expel the germs of wasting disease. In Turkey, the veil has been drawn aside from the face of woman, and, in law, the wife has been awarded the rights which are her Magna Carta under the institution of Christian marriage. That agelong nightmare of perverted romance, the seraglio of the sultans, with the silken cord and secret oubliette, has been thrown open to the whole world as a museum for sightseers.

In the former day, it was not the woman who went to business. It was the business that came to the woman, and a woman's work was never done. An optimist once wrote a little booklet called *Blessed Be Drudgery*, and for most women, this was the only beatitude. A woman was the bearer, not of children alone, but of every burden. While she rocked the cradle, she also gathered sticks for the fire, she drew water from the well. The song of her spinning-wheel yielded woolen thread. On her loom, the thread was woven into cloth. Her arm ground the corn between the upper and the nether millstones. Her hand kneaded the bread. She kept the home and cleaned it of its dust. In truth did the dictionary describe her as the housewife. Morning, noon and night she was wedded to the duties of her domicile.

Today's homework has been greatly relieved by labour-saving appliances. The washing-machine, steam heat, the electric carpet-sweeper, the modern stove—all these and many other devices have helped to preserve the graces and beauty and health of the housewife.

But the greatest change of all lies in the fact that home is no longer a woman's place of business. A girl need no longer marry when she does not love. She has achieved a choice of career. There is the office, the factory, the hotel, the restaurant, the hospital. Women serve as secretaries and typists; as doctors, dentists and nurses; as preachers in the pulpit, professors in the college and teachers in the school; as architects, artists and actresses. The women of today write books, they supervise machinery, they drive automobiles, they pilot airplanes; they play golf and polo and lawn tennis; they travel, they hunt, they fish, they swim, they climb mountains. In the United States there are eight and one-half million women employed in gainful occupations, and women are said to own forty per cent, or two-fifths, of the wealth of the country.

The Decision

Thomas Carlyle has defined human life as a supreme choice between the Everlasting Yea and the Everlasting Nay. It is not enough to declare that, in this twentieth century, the fact of facts is the entrance of women for the first time into their appointed kingdom of opportunity. To conquer a kingdom never has been more than a beginning. The question is always, What is to be done with a kingdom after it has been conquered? We have to keep the trust we have won. Shakespeare says, "A victory is twice itself when the achiever brings home full numbers." Now that woman has come into her own, what are we going to do with the sacred legacy some women have laid down their lives to leave us? The bars have been withdrawn; the gates are flung wide; woman has now to choose between the virtue of an opportunity used and the sin of an opportunity wasted—a kingdom of glorious realization or a kingdom of empty disillusionment.

We talk of the new woman. There is no new woman, there never will be, and there ought to be no old woman. Woman is eternal, and youth is her everlasting heritage. Bury the girl-queen, Ankh-el-en-Amen, with King Tut-an-Khaman, in a grave, four thousand years remote; awaken her from her long last sleep; and we find that her affections, her charm, her tender coquetries, her little vanities, her very perfumes, are expression of woman's personality as we know it today. The woman of the past, and since the dawn of time, generation after generation of women have had to face the decision between the Everlasting yea and the Everlasting Nay, to the will and purpose of God Himself.

To me it has always seemed as if my sisters have borne their full share of whatever blame has had to be distributed. The woman of selfish instincts has been well advertised as the incorrigible temptress of mankind, and if anything goes wrong, the cry has been *"Cherchez la femme."* Adam eats the apple, but it was Eve who handed it to him. Macbeth commits murder, but it was Lady Macbeth who slipped the dagger into his hand. Lured by the song of the sirens, Ulysses only avoids shipwreck on the rocks by sealing the ears of his sailors with wax and having himself bound to the mast of his ship, while Calypso in her cave is the symbol of a lover in every port. It is Helen whose frailty plunges nations into war. It is Delilah whose seductions rob Samson of his manhood. It is Jezebel whose worldliness induces Ahab to worship false gods. It is Cleopatra whose passions involve Mark Antony in ruin. It is Herodias who sacrifices the modesty of her daughter, Salome, to the desire that the head of John the Baptist be handed to her on a charger. To the Moslem, a woman was a body without a soul, and to many a saint of the middle ages, she was an emanation of the Evil One.

But in every age the woman who lives for herself has been overcome by the woman who lives for others.

In every age, there have been countless women who, as exemplars of whatsoever things are true, whatsoever things are honest, whatsoever things are just, whatsoever things are pure, whatsoever things are of good report, sowed the seed of which the womanhood of today is the harvest; and it is for these heroines that man, if he be worth the name, will reserve his honour. Not in vain did Sarah, the leader of all whose home is the covered wagon, follow the patriarch of patriarchs as he wandered, he knew not whither, pitching his tent and building his altars and digging his wells. Not in vain did Rebekah entrust her young life to a lover unseen and inspire her son, through Jacob, a dissembler, to be Israel, the prince. Not in vain did the nameless mother of Moses hide her babe in a cradle of bulrushes and so defend the infant from that mortality, hideous and preventable, which has been inflicted, alas, on myriads of children who never knew of Pharaoh, on the banks of the Nile. Not in vain did Deborah, the prophetess, dispense justice to the people, inspire Barak to resist the oppressor and break forth into a song of triumph that is sung unto this day. Not in vain did Ruth, born a pagan of Moab, cling to her mother-in-law and discover that the path of self-denial may lead by a strange Providence to supreme happiness in the home. Not in vain did Hannah bring the secret sorrows of her being to the tabernacle of all consolation, and, in grateful acknowledgment of God's answer to her prayer, dedicate her boy, Samuel, to the priesthood of the Lord. Not in vain did Anna, the prophetess, herself a widow, wait on the Lord in hope of the Messiah; and not in vain did there arise, in the fullness of all time, the gentle and courageous Maiden of Nazareth, in whose virgin heart there was inspired the Supreme Hope of our salvation, who bore the Christ of God, the Word of Love made Flesh, and by her submission to the pains and toils of Bethlehem and Nazareth, prepared for us our redemption.

The Rejoinder

From time to time we catch the echo of an unworthy and cynical sneer at churches, crowded with women. We are told that a Frenchman only goes to church three times in his life—twice he is carried, once he is led—at his baptism as a babe, his marriage and his funeral; that in each case it is a woman who takes him to the altar, who bears him in her arms, who leads him by the hand, who soothes him in his last sleep. Religion is good enough for women!

I have always thanked the skeptic for that taunt. I

welcome it as the highest compliment that has ever been paid to my sex. For once in his thinking the skeptic is quite right. It is the women who go to church. It is the mothers who pray for their absent sons and daughters. It is the wife who regards her marriage as a sacrament to be blessed by God Himself. For a woman deals not with theories alone, not with art alone, not with science alone, but with the innermost secrets of life itself. She handles the infant limbs of her child. She tends the sick father in his pain and weariness. She feeds the hungry. She soothes the sorrowful. It is, indeed, the supreme triumph of woman that, in all ages, in all countries, she has fostered and safeguarded a faith in God. Often enough, her vision of the unseen has been obscured by circumstances and distorted by superstition, but however defective the eyesight, at least it has not been the blindness of a blank and blasphemous materialism. Women may have believed at times too much. But at least they have avoided the worse evil of believing too little.

For what we call the woman's movement is not social merely, not political merely, not economic merely. It is the direct fulfillment of the gospel of the Redeemer. It was Jesus who taught the world the full lesson of what is meant by chivalry to women. It was he Who, at the well of Samaria, talked with an oft-divorced wife and told her of a God Whom she could worship in spirit and in truth. It was He Who, within the Temple, itself, at Jerusalem, dared to defend a woman, taken in adultery, from her heartless persecutors by saying to man in his hypocrisy, "He that is without sin among you, let him first cast a stone at her." He it was Who visited the little girl on her deathbed and, by the omnipotence of love, called her back to life again. He it was Who likened His Church to a Bride, and Himself to the Bridegroom, drawing from the life of women, their lamps, their pieces of silver for housekeeping, the very broom with which they sweep the house, His immortal parables.

Happy, then, is the woman who realizes, even in these days of enfranchisement, that her life, however abundant it may be, is still hidden in the Christ of God. For it is in Christ that woman is transformed and transfigured by a miracle of redemption. Accustomed to flattery, to ease and to affluence, she breaks her alabaster box of spikenard, very precious, and pours the ointment over His feet, so that the fragrance thereof fills the whole house where they are sitting. Indeed, the woman who had naught save penitence to bring Him, shed her tears also over those same weary feet and wiped them with the hair of her head. Is it the women who go to church? It has not always been to so comfortable a place as church that women have trod the *Via Dolorosa* of a faith that nothing in heaven, nothing in hell itself could shake from its foundations. On that first Good Friday, when all the apostles had forsaken the Crucified Christ and fled from the scene of His redeeming agony, it was the women who were the last seen at the Cross, watching Him there; and on the Morn of Resurrection, when the night was still unlit by the first hint of the brightest dawn in history, the women were not afraid to risk the perils of those riotous streets and make their way, loyally and modestly and reverently, to the silent tomb. It was in the body of a woman that Christ was born; and the souls of women were the cradles of the Church.

Apprenticeship

In that Roman world, three-quarters of the people, men

and women, were slaves. A woman was often illiterate, often maltreated, often unworthy of herself, often frivolous, often the mere toy of the trifler and the worldling. To defend womanhood and to redeem women became, therefore, the most urgent of all the regenerative tasks of the Church. Weak in health, insignificant in appearance, Paul the Apostle would have aroused laughter had he appeared as a knight of the tourney. Yet no knight who ever wore armour and rode with lance in rest, has ever displayed a more reckless audacity in defense of the weak than did St. Paul at Philippi when, with Silas, he stood forth in the open street and rescued a poor, lonely, friendless girl whose pitiable mentality was exploited for gain by her pagan masters. For the sake of that girl, the Apostle to the Gentiles was scourged within an inch of his life; yet, blood–stained, bruised, shackled, incarcerated in a dungeon of utter darkness, he was so utterly transported with joy over her deliverance from the chains of wrong that he joined Silas in hymns of praise which shook the prison like an earthquake.

Few were the women who, at first, were fitted for leadership in the Church; and with a wise common-sense, St. Paul made it clear that the Church was no place for chatter and contention, but that, instead of disturbing public service, women should talk over what they did not understand with their husbands when they returned home. But not long had Christ been risen, not long had he ascended to glory, before there began to be manifest in the Church an attitude towards women wholly new to that of any former generation. There, in the upper room at Jerusalem, the women were present with the Apostles, joining with them in prayer and praise, and waiting with them for the gift of the Holy

Spirit. All of us are familiar with the preaching of Philip the Evangelist, to whose ministry of the Ethiopian eunuch owed his conversion. Most of us forget that, when Paul visited the home of Philip at Cæsarea, he found there four daughters, virgins, who also were preachers. All of us have been told, times without number, about the conversion of the Philippian gaoler, and wonderful, indeed, it was. But it was not the Philippian gaoler, crying out, "What must I do to be saved?" who helped Paul and Silas to found a church in the city. It was a woman named Lydia, who managed her own business. She was a woman who dyed and sold purple fabrics, and as a flower unfolds its petals to the sun, so was it with Lydia, "whose heart the prise which, although of a secular character, was dedicated to the Cross of Christ and became the instrument for the extension of His kingdom.

All of us remember that it was to the inspired pen of St. Paul that mankind has owed *The Epistle to the Romans*—for two thousand years the very foundation of our Christian thinking. But not all of us remember that the messenger by whom that priceless missive was carried to its destination was a woman—"Phoebe, a servant of the church at Cenchrea." In those difficult, troublesome, dangerous, perplexing times, what confidence in her loyalty, her courage, her discretion! Centuries of years before the business man learned the value of a woman as a secretary, the Apostle discerned it, and claimed that value for the greatest and noblest and costliest of all causes.

And did he address his epistle to the great Cathedral of St. Peter? There *was* no Cathedral of St. Peter, and St. Peter had yet to visit Rome. It was to the house of a woman, Priscilla, and her husband, Aquilla, that the priceless epistle was dispatched—that house which was the home of the first Christian Church in the eternal metropolis of the Cæsars.

I know well that the Church, as a whole, whether it be Protestant or Catholic, still persists as a whole in debarring women from the orders of her clergy. Not so the Society of Friends; not so the Salvation Army—communions relatively small in numbers, perhaps. But I would ask where you will find in any fellowship of the Church a more noble witness to the love of God in Christ and to the claims of human justice? Among the Quakers and the Salvationists, wisdom is justified of her daughters as well as her sons.

But I want to say, here, that no law, whether civil or ecclesiastical, has ever availed to exclude my sisters in any generation from that Calendar of the Saints which far transcends the spiritual authority, be it of Pope or cardinal, of bishop, priest or deacon, of minister, elder or any officer of any communion, gathered together in the name of Christ. Wherever there is a "glorious company of the Apostles," wherever there is a "goodly fellowship of the prophets," wherever there is a "noble army of martyrs," there will be found the King's Daughters, all radiant within and clothed with glistening robes of righteousness.

The Glory of Holiness

Exulting in a newly-found freedom, the girlhood of today revels in the rivalries of sport, of audacious exploits in the air, on the earth, amid the waves of the sea, and even of sheer physique—the perfection of form and feature and movement. A woman, a man, created in the image of God, is, in deed, the inspiration of painter and sculptor, the most splendid being, apart from the

Everlasting Father Himself, in this illimitable universe.

But there is no woman, so beautiful in herself, that she may not be beautiful also by the love around her, nor is any woman plain whom love transfigures. The mother bending over her babe, the Red Cross nurse binding up a wound, the Salvation Army lassie kneeling by a penitent—they are all miracles of loveliness. For it is not upon the outward appearance that the love of Christ is lavished in measureless superabundance. That great love is shed abroad in the heart. Hence, it is in the cause of Christ that a girl, even if her countenance is deemed to be homely, discerns a chance and a career, eternal in the never-ending satisfaction. In that Roman world, with its intrigues and jealousies and worship of men's success, Paul declared that there is a loveliness independent of costume, of elaborate braiding of the hair, of extravagant jewelry—the grace of character which languishes not with the years but is enriched even by sorrow, even by suffering. His was the gospel that includes the dandelion in the daisy chain, and in that contest where beauty is holiness, offers the crown that fadeth not away.

Glance over the scroll of history, stained on every page with the shedding of blood and tears, and you will be amazed by the dynasty of sainthood, which women have maintained unbroken. They have been the heroines of home. Over and over again, we read of the Jewish kings that the mother's name was So-and-So, and with that statement there comes the verdict—he did that which was right, or he did that which was wrong, in the eyes of the Lord. Like mother, like son. There, in a small town of Asia Minor, a boy was born whose name is known today wherever language is spoken. To whom did Timothy owe his equipment in life? To his Greek father? No. It was to his Jewish mother, Eunice, and his grandmother, Lois, who instructed him in the Scriptures and prepared him to follow the Apostle Paul to the ends of the earth.

Upon the scroll of history, stained on every page with the shedding of blood and tears, you will find the dynasty of sainthood, which woman has maintained unbroken. Her capability of fiery vehemence, irrevocable resolution of purpose, made her a thousand times the stronger man when facing mortal terror. With the quickness of immediate intuition, the heart of a woman responds to the voice of truth, and truth is the path that she follows. Nor does she falter by the wayside.

Woman has been the heroine of the arena. Side by side with men, our sisters faced the horrors of the amphitheatre, the terrors of the Inquisition, the fearful excesses of the Boxers, and the prolonged fury of the Turk. On the disputed frontiers of Christendom, by the million, they have laid down their lives in defense of purity.

Women have been the heroines of emancipation. Clad in the armour of light, there is always a Jeanne D'Arc to lift her stainless head out of the greed, the lust, the unbelief of the time and captain the armies in a battle for liberty.

As a child, I would sleep with a woman's book under my pillow. As I read that book, I would pray to be made a deliverer of the oppressed. My name, Evangeline, was derived from its pages, and one day, as I shall always remember, I was introduced, as a little girl, to the author of that book. "You are the little woman," said Abraham Lincoln to Harriet Beecher Stowe, "who started this war;" and it was true. While one of God's children wears the chain of servitude, womankind will accept no peace.

They offer themselves as a sacrifice on that altar of purity where death in its most awful forms is preferred to an easy but humiliating dishonour. These are the women who, from their graves, rise to rebuke any woman who surrenders the best in herself to what is unworthy of her womanhood.

The Memory

Why is it that, today, the League of Nations, itself, is engaged upon suppressing the White Slave traffic? It is because there was a woman, Josephine Butler, who, fifty years ago, faced ostracism and calumny in the defense of the defenseless among those sisters of hers in every land, who had been entangled in the shackles of shame.

Women are heroines of service. The spirit which illuminated the life of St. Elizabeth of Hungary, who gave bread to the poor with a grace so tender and tactful that the loaves turned to roses in her hands, never dies. We see Elizabeth Fry in the white bonnet of the Quaker, sitting in the fœtid prisons of an unreformed England. We see Florence Nightingale, the Lady of the Lamp, softly visiting the wards of her military hospitals. The women of service!

Finally, women are heroines of sacrifice. We see Edith Cavell, the friend of her foes, uttering forgiveness as, on that dark morning of awful misunderstanding, she faces the firing squad. We see Madame Curie, cheerfully pursuing those perilous researches into a healing science which have cost her the life that was more to her than her own; and, as I gather together these memories of womanhood in all ages, so glorious in their worldwide and time-defying amplitude, I seem to be led first by one path, then by another, to a shrine of womanhood which, for me, must ever be the most sacred of all. For in my Mother, whose ring I have worn as my talisman of duty and faith and sympathy all these years, I seem to see the heroine who sums up in her person so much of the heroic in others. With her skillful needle, her proved experience of the kitchen, her gentle and loving influence over her husband, my father, William Booth, the Founder of the Salvation Army, and over her eight high-spirited, eager and often mischievous children, she was assuredly a heroine of the home. But in her protest against all that was half-hearted in the Church and iniquitous in the world, she was, not less, a heroine of the arena, a champion of emancipation. Yet was that all? For in her patient devotion to the routine of organization, her astonishing zeal in the preaching of the gospel, her profound respect for the best in human thought and culture, she was a heroine of service. Nor did she escape the crown of martyrdom. For she was condemned to a lingering malady, amid the pangs of which suffering she continued to fulfill her mission, indomitable, the living victory of life over death, incarnate immortality, promoted to everlasting glory.

Truly, it could be said of her, as of the virtuous woman extolled by the Preacher, that her price was above rubies. The heart of her husband did indeed safely trust in her, and she did him good, not evil, all the days of her life. Her candle—a beacon of hope amid despair, of right amid wrong, of love amid sin and shame—went not out by night, however black the night might be, and she stretched forth her hand to the poor; yea, she reached forth her hands to the needy. Strength and honour were her clothing; she did rejoice in the times to come. For she opened her mouth with wisdom and in her tongue was the law of kindness. She looked well to the ways of her household and ate not the bread of idleness. Her children rose up to call her blessed and her husband, known in the gates when he sat among the elders of the land, praised her, saying, "Many daughters have gotten riches, but thou excellest them all." For the riches gathered by my Mother were those treasures in a heaven which neither moth nor rust do corrupt nor thieves break through and steal, the unsearchable riches of Christ.

This sainted Mother of mine was Mother also of the Salvation Army. What she was in herself, a maker of home, a preacher of justice and mercy, a friend of the friendless, a strong hand of help in the dark shadow of despair and shame and sin, that did the Army become, touching human life at many points, and always with the tender touch of healing. In the Salvation Army we see, as it were, the summation of the woman's movement, her equal status with man in social and spiritual and intellectual responsibility, her readiness to find a greater happiness in service than any selfish pleasure could have afforded.

For, if woman has been successful, in inspiring men to great deeds and noble aims, it is because she herself abounds in enthusiasm. It is a mistake to attribute a woman's enthusiasm to excitement, to emotion. It is, rather, an utter abandonment to an aim, only to be carried to triumph by such devotion. *If a woman loves, she worships. If she champions a cause, she will fight for it. If she gives, she gives all. If she lives for, she will die for.*

My Mother was an enthusiast. While retiring and blessed with that conservativeness that always has at its demand perfect control, she abounded in enthusiasm.

The Salvation Army has revealed its spirit, its love, its sincerity, to the peoples of the world more than anything else through the service of its enthusiastic women. The world does not say of us that we possess much, or that we look much, or that we dress much, or that we talk much (unless it is I); but the world has been kind enough to recognize that we love "not in word, but in deed"—achieved in the passion of the Cross.

Shallow and fickle, the mind of the public, bewildered by multitudinous impressions, is apt to seize upon some symbol, some sensation, and to suppose that this is the whole of the affair. Many people think that the women of the Salvation Army are lassies who, in the main, spend their time and energies on waving the tambourine and shouting their "Hallelujahs." During the War, our girls achieved a reputation scarcely less embarrassing. It was supposed that their whole energies were devoted to serving out the doughnuts to the boys in the trenches and gaily welcoming bombardment as a short cut to glory.

Of the courage of our women officers, I would be the last person in the whole world to utter a word of depreciation. 'Tis conscience that makes cowards of us all, and if shell fire no longer alarms, it is because hell fire has lost its terrors.

But death and danger had not been the only trial of these women's faith. They had faced dirt, they had handled disease, they had not flinched before uttermost degradation, they had not been dismayed by the most awful defacements of God's image, imprinted on our race; there is no depth of misery, of despair, of iniquity that is concealed from the steady eyes of the women of the Salvation Army. The hospitals and homes for mothers, deserted by those who should have been at their side as partners in parenthood, the hotels for working women, the visitation of women in prisons, the bureaus of employment, the young women's residences, and the Home League in every corps for helping women to be better housewives, these are only some of the agencies which are conducted by the women officers of the Salvation Army.

Our Citizenship

To my sisters in every land I would say, then, that, today, ours is a great heritage, handed down to us from distant ages. In Ur of the Chaldees, the archaeologist has uncovered the bones of women who, in scores, were slain in order to add a fearful tragedy to the obsequies of a heathen king. If their lives were not their own, are we to say that, claimed by the constraining love of Christ, we shall withhold our lives? I cannot believe that the custom of a cruel despotism is stronger than the call of a crucified Redeemer.

For, believe me, it is not enough for us who are women to go to business. There is the question whether we mean business when we get there. The business of woman, as of man, includes not a productive industry alone, not the professions alone, not the home alone, but citizenship. In the annals of monarchy, what sovereigns have excelled the greatness of woman? The heroism of Boadicea, the patriot queen of Britain, and of Zenobia, the patriot queen of Palmyra, prepares us for a Queen Elizabeth, and Queen Victoria. Yet it is astonishing that the very countries where woman has sat on the throne, long denied to her the rights of the ballot-box. When the World War broke out, there were only four countries where women exercised the suffrage.

But today, what a change! At this moment, the Union of South Africa is the only Dominion within the English-speaking world, American and British, where women do not exercise the suffrage. Even in India, there are women who vote, and in Great Britain the women voters are in a majority over the men. In numerous other countries— Germany, Russia, Czecho-Slovakia, the Netherlands, Sweden, Austria, Hungary, to mention only a few of them—women have won their civic rights as electors and share with men the supreme responsibilities of democracy.

The vote is at once a weapon and a symbol. It enables woman to influence law and policy and progress. It means that women today sit not only on thrones, but in legislatures and cabinets. They are governors of states, they are mayors of cities. They are judges and magistrates on the bench. They are lawyers, who plead causes; they serve on juries which decide them; they are permanent officials. They are even enrolled on the police. In the Red Army of Russia, women, like the Amazons, are recruited as soldiers, and modern war means that, in the making of munitions, the woman's fingers are essential.

Hitherto, we have been able to say that man governed a world where slaves suffered in the sweatshop, where soldiers by the million were slaughtered in the trenches; where slums disgraced the cities; where the saloon and the pawnshop flourished in pitiless partnership; where children were denied education and life itself; where gilded vice was tolerated and shameful poverty condoned. But we women have now the vote. We women have now the voice. We women have now the property. We women have now the handling of our own careers. If today there is a war, if today there is drink, if today there is vice, if today there is poverty, God Who has called us into His kingdom will not hold us guiltless.

A Monument

Of all the monuments ever raised by the hand of man, and adorned with the art of his intellect, and consecrated with the reverence of his soul, the loveliest is a memorial to a woman. With slender minarets for sentinels and soaring cupola for canopy, the Taj Mahal, pale as a countenance, yet delicately responsive to the rose of dawn and eve, rises in exquisite perfection, a poem in marble and mosaic, saying to the heavens themselves what no language has ever uttered—lonely, unapproachable and serene.

Yet I am inclined to think that I could mention another memorial, nearer home than the Taj Mahal in India, which, when all the books are opened and the secrets of all hearts are known, would surpass even the masterpiece of Shah Jehan in the marvel of its worldwide, its agelong significance. The most respendent of temples, built with hands, so said our Lord, would be outglorified by a shrine in which the edifice is of living stones, eternal in the heaven of human happiness. Architecture, however superb, if dedicated to perpetual silence, is not enough. Sorrow is sanctified, not by silence alone, but by service.

Here in New York, the husband of a wonderful wife has consecrated his irreparable loss to a glorious gain. The hostelry for womanhood which John Markle has entrusted to the Salvation Army is no mausoleum, however magnificent, but a home for the homeless, a refuge for the tempted, a haven for the perplexed, a comradeship for the lonely, a joyous palace of loving pardon, of gracious hope, of inspiring appeal, of tender sympathy and of resolute consecration. The lifelong memories of the generous benefactor are, as it were, incarnate in the smiles and laughter, the games and friendships of girls, who little think of the price, paid in bereavement, for their healthful, wholesome environment.

All the world, as Omar Khayyam has sung, is but a "battered caravanserai;" for too many millions of homeless wanderers, a comfortless place of passage. We women have made many homes in the world. But we have now the task of changing the world into a home. We have seen many fathers of families. We have now to realize the Fatherhood that includes all families, the Fatherhood of God in Christ. The housekeeping that we have not to undertake is housekeeping on the grand scale; it must include all nations, all people in a nation, the rich and the poor, the saints and the sinners—come ye to the waters; come and be reconciled to God in His heaven and man upon earth.

The Two Ideals

The eternal choice—how it confronts us! We cannot escape it—we must decide. A girl stood in the temple of Diana—a gracious, winning girl, lovely in her fresh young womanhood. Her lover was at her side, pleading on his face; he touched her hand, and it was a persuasive touch. Would she not concede one little pinch of incense to the goddess whose altar rose before her? Just a matter of form; but she refused. Christ or Diana? It meant Christ.

Amid our education, our wealth, our luxuries, our athletics, our emancipation from restraints and prejudices, our opportunities, there arises, once more, the question of questions—to whom do we owe our ultimate allegiance? Christ or something less than Christ, something lower than Christ, something less loving, less wise, less strong than Christ?

"Ah, my God,
What might I not have made of Thy fair world,
Had I but loved Thy highest creature here?
It was my duty to have loved the highest;
It surely was my profit had I known;
It would have been my pleasure had I seen.
We needs must love the highest when we see it,
Not Lancelot, nor another."

To my sisters, the wide world over, I make my appeal. "We needs must love the highest when we see it; not Lancelot, nor another."

In that immortal vision of the future, here and hereafter, which we owe to the inspired genius of St. John the Divine, we are shown two pictures of womanhood, each a contrast to the other. We have the *Woman Who Gets All She Can* and the *Woman Who Gives All She Has;* the woman whose love is concentrated on herself and the woman whose love is consecrated to others.

About the *Woman Who Gets,* there was terrible fascination. "When I saw her," wrote John, "I wondered with great admiration." There she was, proudly seated on a scarlet beast, herself arrayed in purple, and decked with gold, precious stones and pearls; in her uplifted hand she held a golden cup. For her, there was merchandise of fine linen, and silk, and ivory, and brass, and cinnamon, and odours, and ointments, and frankincense, and wine, and oil, and fine flour of wheat. The *Woman Who Gets* could order what she liked. She could command the trade of the world, and rich argosies crossed the ocean at her behest. For her pleasure, her entertainment, her luxury, her convenience, she could summon to her bidding her horses and chariots and her slaves. She was mistress even of "the souls of men." The *Woman Who Gets* was a woman for whom men do sell their very souls.

Brilliant, successful, photographed, flattered, pursued by publicity, the *Woman Who Gets* obtains her reward. Yet amid all her glitter of jewels, her changes of raiment, her array of luxury, she lives in a false glare from a nether world. What use had the *Woman Who Gets* for the company of saints and martyrs? All that she desired was to reign with the kings of the earth, to enter the most exclusive society, whatever the moral tone, to be married to the man with the highest title or greatest fortune, whatever his moral character; to live in the largest house, by whatever means it is paid for. Do not suppose that she is always to be found among the wealthy. In factories and offices and restaurants, you will also recognize the *Woman Who Gets,* who accepts gifts from the man she intends to discard; the golddigger, who plays on the frailties of another woman's husband; the wife who asks no questions when her husband, from some mysterious source, finds the money for her fur coat and new motor car—the goddess at whose pagan shrine men burn that incense, the price of which is banditry, bootlegging, graft and a reckless speculation on Wall Street. The *Woman Who Gets* is the woman who asks of others what others have no right to obtain for her.

"A great wonder," also, to St. John the Divine was the *Woman Who Gives;* and in her case it was a wonder in heaven. She is the woman who, wherever she goes, brings heaven with her, a queen of happiness. There we see her, clothed with the sun, a radiant being whose whole life is lived in the light of a great joy. With the moon under her feet, she knows no shadow of jealousy, of selfishness, of anger, as she advances to meet us, nor has she need of jewels, for in her crown there shine twelve stars, beacons that proclaim her kindly purposes, her tender thoughts, her reverent prayers, her patient hopes. Such is the *Woman Who Gives,* who hears the call of the race, whatever it be, and obeys it, whatever it costs, even unto the agony of the motherhood which transforms every woman into a Madonna.

The Supreme Sacrifice

It was in the month of February, a few brief years ago. The thermometer registered fifteen below zero. The wind was blowing sixty-five miles an hour. A boat, the *Larchmont,* drew out from its crib at Boston, and it was midnight. Among its precious cargo of human souls were eleven Salvation Army women, coming to attend an annual Congress I was conducting in New York. The eldest had not seen more than twenty-three summers. Therefore the little company were young and fair, and enthusiastic in their ambition for a future of service in the Kingdom of God under our banners.

Musically gifted, as is the blessed wont of the Scandinavian people, immediately upon leaving the shore they gathered around the piano in the salon. The vote was cast for that great favourite, the hymn of their fathers, expressive of the faith in which their mothers had reposed an unfailing trust: *Rock of Ages, Cleft for Me.*

Time, as always when in company with music, was forgotten. The lowering of a heavy fog was unnoticed.

Many hymns were sung. Then back to the old favourite, and the voices echoed through the narrow passageways of the vessel, lifted above the throb of the propellors and the boom of the rising billows . . .

> *"While I draw this fleeting breath,*
> *When mine eyes shall close in death,*
> *When I rise to worlds unknown,"*

so sang the women who gave . . .

Crash! Crowded gangways. The screams of women who fainted. Little children dragged from beds. Mothers, with babies in their arms, caught in the jam. Fathers striking blindly at the air in helpless efforts to help. Billows stamping death-threatening heels over the decks. Winds howling through the rigging. The gunwales shattered. The boat badly listing, and in the hurry, a *scarcity of lifebelts.*

Eleven Salvation Army girls are standing on the deck of the sinking vessel. Their little blue skirts spread to the hurricane. Their bonnets are thrown back from their fair faces. Their hair tangled in the fingers of the high wind. Their eyes lifted to a starless sky. Their hands clasped in each other's, forming an immortal chain to bind the hearts of the saints. "Oh," said one, to a man who wanted her to take his lifebelt, "we can die better than you can. For us to go down, is to go up," and together they challenged the wide, wild deep: "O death, where is thy sting? O grave, thy victory?" and flung the Salvation Army's battlecry around the world! *We live not unto ourselves. Others!*

And so may I use this solemn memory in the spirit of our Lord and Saviour Whom I love, with faith in Him Whom I claim my Pardon, my Prophet, my Priest, and King. In the Gospel of Christ as I have received it, in the spirit of my religion as I teach it, may I as that we all link hands in a solemn contract to press on. We must light new lamps. We must tread new paths. We must go on. While a neglected child cries, we must go on. While there is a land to Christianize, we must go on. While a lost girl wanders, we must go on. While there is a city or a home without a Bible, we must go on. Wherever the ship of life is in danger, there—death or life—must we go on!

Of us, may it ever be true that

> *"we have chosen our path_*
> *Path to a clear purposed goal,*
> *Path of advance!"*

May we ever be dedicated wholly to Him

> *"who unwillingly sees*
> *One of His little ones lost."*

Of all who hear that call to service, to sacrifice, to the only victory, worth the winning, mankind will ever declare from its burdened yet grateful heart:

> *"Ye, like angels, appear,*
> *Radiant with ardour divine!*
> *Beacons of hope, ye appear!*
> *Languor is not in your heart,*
> *Weakness is not in your word,*
> *Weariness not on your brow.*
> *Ye alight in our van! At your voice,*
> *Panic, despair, flee away.*
> *Ye move through the ranks, recall*
> *The stragglers, refresh the outworn,*
> *Praise, reinspire the brave!*
> *Order, courage, return.*
> *Eyes rekindling, and prayers,*

Follow your steps as ye go.
Ye fill up the gaps in our files,
Strengthen the wavering line,
'Stablish, continue our march,
On, to the bound of the waste,
On, to the City of God."

Kay F. Rader

Kay F. Rader

Commissioner Kay F. Rader is the former World President of Women's Organizations for The Salvation Army. She and her husband, Paul A. Rader, who was elected the 15th General of The Salvation Army in July, 1994, served as international leaders until July, 1999, when they were officially retired and returned to their homeland, the United States of America.

The Raders served 22 years in Korea. Fluent in the language, they were engaged in teaching and training, as well as carrying major administrative responsibilities during their latter years of service in that country. Commissioner Rader conducted schools of prayer throughout Korea and in the United States. Her life and ministry are marked by her experience of prayer, life in the Spirit, and a commitment to help women realize their full potential in ministry and mission.

Commissioner Rader holds honorary Doctor of Divinity degrees from Asbury Theological Seminary and Roberts Wesleyan College and the degree of Doctor of Humane Letters from Greenville College. She serves as a member of the Board of Trustees of Asbury Seminary and Roberts Wesleyan College. She is active in the movement to contain the spread of pornography and its harms to children and families. She has tirelessly championed the welfare of women and children worldwide.

Daughter of retired Methodist minister, Rev. J. O. Fuller, and graduate of Asbury College, Commissioner Rader taught public school before becoming an officer. She is an avid reader, enthusiastic runner, and devoted wife, mother and grandmother. The Raders have three married children, Edie, J. P., and Jennie, and seven grandchildren.

❧ Keeping the Dream Alive ❧
By Kay F. Rader

KAMPALA, UGANDA—*It was just past midday when we spotted the four seated together on a rocky ledge that formed part of the hotel garden. Sensing the approach of strangers, they huddled close, but still gave us incredibly broad, beautiful smiles.*

I wondered about our finding children here in the garden on a weekday, so when we drew near enough I greeted them. "Hi! How are you? Do you go to school?"

"We are girls," they shot back, turning aside as if to elude the shock on my face. Then, looking out into nowhere, murmured, "Mamas don't send girls to school."

CONGO, KINSHASA—*Dutifully following the doctor who is our guide at a Salvation Army clinic, we find ourselves in a very large room lined with beds. In each bed lies a young woman who remains very still and extraordinarily quiet as we speak in hushed tones with members of staff.*

The next stop appears to be a delivery room.

"So, does this mean the women we have just seen were in labor?" I ask.

"That is correct," replies the doctor. "And no one made a sound?"

"No one." He continues, "When in labor, African women make only one sound. It can be heard at the very moment of birth."

Then comes the final, most discomfiting statement: "African women have learned to suffer in silence."

MUMBAI (BOMBAY), INDIA—*On the way to the airport, our taxi is stopped by traffic police, the driver is asked to step outside, and we are left to wait in the car. Within seconds, the car is surrounded. Sad, haunting eyes of children as young as four—mere babies—stare through the glass windows. They beg, even as they struggle to balance emaciated infants on their hips. In the distance, women (their mothers perhaps?) crouch beside the dusty road, feverishly chopping, toiling laboriously for the prospect of a mere morsel of food per family member. Home for these women is the small area in which they move about; their only shelter is the sky. Privacy is an unknown concept, certainly never experienced by the likes of these women. To them, even a small candle to dispel the darkness at nightfall is beyond imagination.*

"What is life for those women?" I muse.

Our colleague, Indian by birth, responds, "Terrible." Then he says, "In India, they say a woman born into poverty is twice oppressed. Her first oppression is that she is born woman. But to be born poor as a woman adds another oppression all its own."

Evangeline Booth, in her days as commander of The Salvation Army in the United States, believed transformation for women was imminent. Contrast the scenes from Uganda, Kinshasa and Mumbai with the tone of her lecture, "Woman," in which she announces "the emergence of womanhood in this year of grace, 1930. . . ." With unbounded optimism, she speaks of girls from West to East, North to South,

> *life pulsating in their veins, gathered into schools and colleges, to develop their powers, spiritual, mental and physical, and the more abundant life, which they were created to love.*

. . . There is no country in the world where women, however ill-used, however illiterate, are not beginning, at least to think about the long overdue chance of going to business.[1]

Seventy years later, at the beginning of the 21st century, any similarity between Evangeline's portrait and that of women facing the new millennium is barely discernible. Today's picture casts dark and lengthening shadows upon women's "imminent" achievement of unbarred emergence into "abundant life." Indeed, in many cultures today, the status of womanhood may be appropriately described as both lowly and lonely.

In the Libby Purves novel, *More Lives Than One,* pretty, 20-year-old Anna Melville visits modern Egypt. There she discovers the double lowliness of being a foreigner and a woman.

Coming from a nation, class and generation of pretty young women who had little doubt about their own status, she found it interesting and even piquant to be discounted thus. At last she was sharing the experience of most of the world's women: slumming it for awhile in the sisterhood of ignored females. It would be something to remember, like the pyramids.[2]

The sadness lies in our knowing that Egypt cannot be considered exceptional. The truth is, gender discrimination is universal. And in any culture, such a dead-end street can terminate only in dire circumstances.

Education

"The world tells us what we are to be," says one young African woman, "and shapes us by the ends it sets before

---

[1] Evangeline Booth, "Woman," Fleming H. Revell Company: New York, 1930, p.8.

[2] Libby Purves, More Lives Than One, Hodder and Stoughton Publishing Company: London, 1998, p. 1.

us; the less a woman has in her head, the lighter she is for carrying." *Mamas don't send girls to school!* According to United Nations reports, females without literacy skills face dark futures of dependency. Many girls are heading for such a future. Of the more than 130 million 6- to 11- year- olds who are not in school in the developing world, nearly two-thirds are girls.[3]

The fact is that countries that allow women to remain illiterate create unnecessary hurdles to economic development. The UN reports make clear the necessity of gender-sensitive education, as well as increased job opportunities. Dr. Eddah Gachukia, executive director of the Forum for African Women Educationalists (FAWE), observes, "Girls must not only be educated, they must also be accorded the opportunity to use their education and their skills to make decisions about and be participants in the development of Africa."[4]

Health

Where is the person who does not aspire to be the perfect picture of health? But the cumulative picture for women worldwide is anything but perfect; in fact, it is alarming. *The Progress of Nations, 1996,* reveals what was happening to the health, nutrition, and education of children in the late 20th century. Beginning with one of many tragedies, that of maternal mortality and morbidity, editor Peter Adamson reports that the number of women who die each year in pregnancy and childbirth is close to 600,000. Answers to the burning question,

---

[3] *Facts and Figures 1998,* United Nations Children's Fund (UNICEF), New York City. See www.unicef.org.
[4] "Education," *State of the World's Children 1999,* UNICEF, New York City. See www.unicef.org/SOWC99

"How can such a heavy burden of death, disease, and disability have continued for so long with so little outcry?" are found in what this commentary calls a "conspiracy of silence" and a "failure of imagination" by women who are conditioned not to complain but to cope.[5]

The World Guide's Millennium Edition, 1999–2000, indicates that in some countries, female infants are killed outright; in others, girl babies are simply fed less well and receive little health care. Cultural eating practices often result in girls as well as their mothers dining last and consuming the least amount of food in the family. In addition, fewer visits to health clinics make girls susceptible to sickness and stunted growth. In many cultures, girls are even denied access to sun and fresh air, which makes them vulnerable to illness.[6] Those conditions lead to a higher mortality rate for females than for males (the world average is 111 girls to every 100 boys). In the 15 to 40 age bracket, 75 per cent more women die than men.

As if women did not have enough to contend with, multibillion-dollar illegal sex markets ensnare millions of children each year, the majority of them in Asia. These children are at high risk of contracting sexually transmitted diseases, including HIV/AIDS. Calling this problem, "Girls as Goods," Laura Montgomery, a professor of sociology and anthropology, states that while the total number of children involved in the sex trade worldwide is unknown, there is evidence that the number of girls involved is increasing in Europe, Africa, and Latin

---

[5] Peter Adamson, "A Failure in Imagination," *The Progress of Nations,* UNICEF House: New York, 1996, pp. 2–7.

[6] *The World Guide 1999/2000: An Alternative Reference on the Countries of Our Planet: Millennium Edition,* Garamond Press: Aurora, Ontario, Canada, 1999. Facts obtained from ni@newint.org

America. Most are girls ages 6 to 16, who suffer from many health problems as a result. Reports indicate, for example, that in Thailand, almost 50 percent of child prostitutes are HIV-positive.[7]

In the minds of people in certain cultures, female genital mutilation (FGM) provides a way to keep young women from being victimized in these ways. A tradition designed to preserve virginity, ensure marriageability, and contain sexuality, FGM is common practice in many countries. Approximately 2 million girls are mutilated every year. In Djibouti and Somalia, 98 percent of girls are mutilated.[8]

Welfare

Even before a girl child is born, prenatal testing to determine the gender of the fetus may be used to deselect, or abort her. Girls who are not aborted may be strangled, poisoned, buried in the sand of the desert, thrown into the sea, exposed in the jungle, fed to sharks, or drowned in milk with a prayer they will return as sons. Girl babies not killed at birth may be allowed to die by starvation or sheer neglect. As a result, inordinate numbers of girls born worldwide are simply unaccounted for.

Girls who do survive face other hardships. *The State of the World's Children, 1998,* reports that women, on average, put nearly twice the hours men do into family and household maintenance. In Bangladesh, India and Nepal, for example, girls and women spend three to five hours more a week than do boys and men performing

---

[7] Laura Montgomery, "Girls as Goods: The Problem of Child Prostitution," *Together: A Journal of World Vision International,* January–March 1996, pp. 7-9.

[8] Nabial Toubia, "Sources, FGM," *Progress of Nations,* UNICEF House: New York, 1996, pp. 6, 7.

tasks such as carrying fuel and growing and processing food. Girls and women then spend an additional 20 to 30 hours a week performing other unpaid household tasks.[9]

Poverty still has a woman's face. UNICEF's *Facts and Figures, 1998,* reveals that of an estimated 1.3 billion people worldwide living in poverty, more than 70 percent are women and girls. This report is a reminder that as the world seeks sustainable growth and a peaceful future, women's full equality and participation in all spheres of life are essential. Yet women continue to face profound discrimination, barriers to advancement, denial of rights, and low wages. (Women's wages worldwide range from 50% to 80% of men's wages).[10]

Gender Inequality

Of the many issues influencing the adolescent experience—the countless, unspoken cultural rules that govern the behavior of females and males in every country on earth, almost from the day they are born—none is more profound than gender.

In many parts of the world, girls face deep prejudices and are denied basic rights to nutrition, health care, education, equality, and often survival itself. Girls marrying in their teens face a number of disadvantages and risks. They typically have less schooling and are more dependent on and subordinate to their partners than girls who marry later, and death rates are higher for both teen mothers and their babies.

---

[9] *The State of the World's Children,* UNICEF, Oxford University Press: London, p. 29.
[10] "Women," *Facts and Figures 1998,* UNICEF, New York City. (Facts found at pubdoc@unicef.org.)

In a contribution to the Salvation Army's United Kingdom Territory *War Cry* of Sept. 6, 1997, Charlotte Bunch of UNICEF stated, "Roughly 60 million women who should be alive today are 'missing' because of gender discrimination, predominantly in south and west Asia, China and North Africa. One quarter to one half of women worldwide suffer physical abuse at the hands of an intimate partner; more than 5,000 women are killed each year in India alone because of inadequate dowries."[11]

A woman cries for help and nobody hears. Her pain is seldom shared because no one knows. She is one who weeps, one who wonders, "Where were they when we cried?"

Salvation Army Response

Lt. Colonel Birgitte Brekke, associate commanding officer in the Bangladesh Command of The Salvation Army, expresses great urgency about settling gender issues. Standing alongside a host of others who are ready and willing to make the effort against all odds, she writes:

> *We live and work in a culture where women are rated second-class citizens. Girls are taught to behave in ways which will show that they are submissive and inferior to their male counterparts. Boys are taught to be strong, independent and self-confident, girls to be demure, adjusting and obedient. Girls are deprived of proper nutrition, health care and education. They are often victims of physical and mental torture and general neglect. When girls are sexually abused in the most terrible way, they are often punished instead of the boys who committed the crime. Daily we read in the newspapers about housewives beings beaten to death by their husbands. Young*

---

[11] Charlotte Bunch, "Women Suffer the World Over," *The War Cry,* No. 6314, The Salvation Army United Kingdom Territory: London, 1997, pp. 4, 5.

girls have acid thrown in their faces by former boyfriends—dis-
figuring them and causing them so much pain it is beyond
words. A growing number of girls are married between the ages
of 8-13 years. Women are longing for freedom, acceptance and
respect. It is in this setting we live and work. It is in this culture
we preach the word of God. We have a message that is the exact
opposite of what is culturally acceptable, a message alien to the
culture, but a message that is so much needed.

Advocates of such counterculture message must have credibility. "Research into gender issues in organizations highlights the different ways in which women and men are able to balance the work of production and repro-duction—i.e., remunerated work, and unpaid work that goes on within the home," say gender specialists Fenella Porter, Ines Smyth and Caroline Sweetman. "Transforming the lives of women living in poverty will not come about until male biases inherent in our organ-izations are identified and addressed."[12]

Catherine Booth, co-founder of The Salvation Army, laid an egalitarian foundation for the Salvation Army movement when she proclaimed the empowering mes-sage of the Gospel for women. Christine Parkin, in her contribution to the book, *Catherine Booth: Her Continuing Relevance,* recalls how the absolute equali-ty of men and women forms the cornerstone of Catherine Booth's thought.

Women were denied every other public office—from a mis-
taken notion of what the Bible taught about women; that
Eve's first bite of the apple and its place in the whole tragedy
of human depravity had created a profound sense of inferi-

---

[12] Fenella Porter, Ines Smyth, and Caroline Sweetman, April–June 2000, "Gender Works: Oxfam's Experience in Policy and Practise," *Together, A Journal of the World Vision Partnership,* Gender and Development, pp. 10-11.

*ority so that the words subjection and submission had both
a social and a religious connotation. Catherine Booth accept-
ed that the Fall had put women into subjection as a consequence of sin and that submission to the male was God's
judgment upon her disobedience. But, she argued, to leave it
there is to reject the good news of the gospel. The grace of
Christ restores what sin had taken away, so that both men
and women can now know the bliss of union with God and
with one another as God had fully intended it to be.*[13]

The Army's view of women affirms their equal dignity and worth as *persons made in the image and likeness of God himself.* When God created humankind, he
made them in the likeness of God. "Male and female he
created them. . . ." (Genesis 1:27). "In Christ you are all
children of God through faith . . . Abraham's offspring,
heirs according to the promise" (Galatians 3:26, 29).
Both women and men were created for His glory. "I will
bring everyone—my sons from far away and my daughters . . . everyone . . . whom I created for my glory, whom
I formed and made" (Isaiah 43:7).

Catherine Booth established a Bible-based rejection of
all forms of gender discrimination. Indeed she is said to
have been a mother who ground into her boys the idea
that their sisters were just as capable and intelligent as
they were. She believed all people are made in the image
of God, that all are heirs of God, that all are joint heirs with
Jesus Christ, and that it was Christ's principle to put
woman on the same platform as man.

The War Cry for Aug. 14, 1880, recorded a Wesleyan
Conference address given by William Booth, the founder
of The Salvation Army and Catherine's husband, in

---

[13] Christine Parkin, "A Woman's Place," in *Catherine Booth, Her
Continuing Relevance* (Clifford Kew, ed.), The Campfield Press: St. Albans
VT., 1990, pp. 11-12.

which he enunciated principles that had characterized the success of the movement. The fourth principle was: *"We employ women."* He went on to recount the remarkable contribution being made by women officers and soldiers to the growth and development of the Army.[14] From its earliest days, the Army's position on women in ministry has been clean and unequivocal. The Salvation Army finds no place for gender discrimination within its beliefs and practices. Whatever biases male-dominated cultures dictate, the Army's commitment is to the empowerment of both women and men in ways consistent with the teachings and example of Christ.

The Culture of Silence

In the stage play, *A Man for All Seasons,* a character known as Mr. Common Man pops from behind the curtain from time to time and speaks directly to the audience. In the climactic scene, Sir Thomas More lays his head on the guillotine, the theatre lights go out, and the blade drops. Then Mr. Common Man says to a stunned audience, "I'm breathing. . .Are you breathing too? It's nice, isn't it? It isn't difficult to keep alive, friends—just don't make trouble— or if you must make trouble, make the sort of trouble that's expected. . .[15] (Bolt, 1960: 162, 163).

Embodied in this speech is the condition of women in the world. Knowing they'd best not make trouble, or if they do, they'd best make only that trouble which is expected, the majority of women succumb. They join a "culture of silence." Like the Congolese women who learn not to make a sound in labor, women in many parts

---

[14] William Booth, "Wesleyan Conference Address," *The War Cry,* The Salvation Army, 1880.

[15] Robert Bolt, A man for All Seasons, Random House, Inc.: New York, 1962, pp. 162, 163.

of the world have been socialized to accept and endure pain in silence. *Living Letters,* a report of visits to the Churches during the Ecumenical Decade (from Churches in Solidarity with Women), states emphatically, "Women . . . accept great injustices, including violence, in silence. Whether because of shame or guilt, or fear—that they will not be believed, or will be blamed, or will lose their dignity—or out of fear of reprisals, or uncertainty . . . loyalty to a cause, to their family, community, or church—whatever the reasons, women often refuse to 'admit' that they have suffered violence."[16]

Women can be silenced by threats or acts of intimidation. Often they are interrupted by men who tell a woman's story and then rationalize away her experience. In far too many places, women are confined to the home and understood to be chattel or pieces of property, not the free creation that God intended. All too often, women are restrained by cultural practices impervious to the gracious impulse of the Spirit and Word.[17]

In the face of all this evidence, there are still Christians who honestly believe that the portrayal of women as "victims" is an exaggeration of women's suffering trumped up by secular feminists; that it is a denial of the many advances that have been made in recognition of women's rights. While it may be true that Western women entering the 21st century have power, education, and privilege unprecedented in human history, there is inarguable proof that inferiority, poverty, injustice, violence, and powerlessness continue to victimize the majority of women worldwide.

The Salvation Army must not be complacent about

---

[16] *Living Letters,* World Council of Churches: Geneva, Switzerland, 1997.
[17] Ibid.

this victimization; rather, it must take arms against it, and enlist women in the fight. During the January 1999 South Asia regional conference held in Colombo, Sri Lanka, Colonel Mary Rajakumari, territorial president of women's organizations, took a firm stance when she delivered an impassioned plea for major paradigm shifts concerning gender issues. She said:

> *Women can no longer passively accept their fate as victims of historical accident or even externally imposed change. All must be involved themselves in the shaping of a new and better world. To ensure this development, women must lead in the direction of change. Women must initiate and implement agendas, aimed at transformation that serve the needs and priorities of the poorest of the poor, the neediest of the needy, most of whom are women!*

Modern studies show that community development efforts fail when the role of women in the social and economic life of the community is ignored; the same efforts succeed when women's needs are addressed. It was Mahatma Ghandi who said, "India has tried to fly with one wing, and she has gone round in circles."

Fighting Convention with the Sword of Truth

Salvation Army women today face gender issues in the light of a new set of values and societal conventions. Advances in biblical scholarship are aiding the efforts of resolving gender issues. Women today should be able to find once-and-for-all answers to the concerns people express about women in ministry, for example. Revisiting traditional interpretations of various problem texts are authors such as Catherine Clark Kroeger *(I Suffer Not a Woman: Rethinking I Timothy 2:11-15 in Light of Ancient Evidence)* and Aida Besancon Spencer, *(Beyond the Curse: Women Called to Ministry)*. Not only do these professionals possess the essential educational credentials to deal with the text, they also have the ability to look beyond traditional male perspectives as they examine the relevant gender issues. The Army's theological position on gender equality, grounded in its historical roots, stands to be fortified by this growing body of women theologians and biblical scholars.

"There is neither Jew nor Gentile, slave nor free, male nor female, for we are all one in Christ Jesus." (Galatians 3:28). Writes Philip Yancey, "Jesus moved the emphasis from God's holiness (exclusive) to God's mercy (inclusive). Instead of the message, 'No undesirables allowed,' He proclaimed, 'In God's Kingdom there are no undesirables.'"[18]

Some would agree. But unfortunately, some still hold to a Puritan view concerning gender issues. In *Catherine Booth: Her Continuing Relevance,* Christine Parkin writes, "The Puritans were not lovers of women's liberty! They believed that women's place was in the home and their duties were circumscribed—submission to the male was absolute. Puritanism's greatest poet, Milton, expressed this position in Samson Agonistes:

> *Therefore God's universal law*
> *Gave to the man despotic power*
> *Over his female in due awe;*
> *Nor from that right to part an hour,*
>
> *Smile she or lour...*
> *He for God only,*
> *She for God in him.*[19]

---

[18] Philip Yancey, *The Jesus I Never Knew,* Zondervan Publishing House: Grand Rapids, Mich., 1995, p. 155.
[19] Parkin, in *Catherine Booth: Her Continuing Relevance,* p. 3.

This brings us to the problematic text, I Timothy 2:12, which has been a great stumbling block for many believers. According to authors Catherine and Richard Kroeger, the problem for these Christians is "whether women are called to silence or to service."[20] This particular issue remains unsettled for many, including not a few Salvationists. Such ambivalence may be at the root of negative attitudes, discrimination, and prejudices within the Army regarding a woman's calling to ministry and her role in leadership. The bias may tend to be passive or subtle as opposed to active or overt, but it is nevertheless a continuing hindrance to Kingdom-building. Prejudice, however slight or unpremeditated, serves no one positively and produces unforgettably painful experiences.

Women and men are called to give all—gifts, talents, training, intelligence, and aptitude—to the service of Christ. Both women and men need to wrestle with the apparently contradictory texts that act as a deterrent, and earnestly seek to discover appropriate resolutions. Once they are committed and willing to alter their bias or personal point of view, differences begin to dissolve, making progress possible.

Both progress and change in this new millennium are facts of life, but to some this may indicate the tearing apart of the very fabric of life, the reweaving of society in ways they neither understand or appreciate. Those living within the period 1900-2025, a period economic analysts are calling the "hinge of history," have faced and will face inordinate challenges. But we must take hope and see an unlimited horizon ahead. Our challenges—

---

[20] Richard Clark and Catherine Clark Kroeger, *I Suffer Not a Woman: Rethinking I Timothy 2:11-15 in Light of Ancient Evidence,* Baker Book House: Grand Rapids, Mich., 1992, p. 13.

not least among them the issues surrounding women's place in society, the church, and the world—must be seen as serviceable tools rather than insurmountable obstacles.

As part of progress, our future will require new understandings about the intrinsic differences as well as the similarities between men and women. People who call themselves feminists have sometimes espoused contradictory positions. One group insists that women and men are equal in every way and another asserts adamantly that women are innocents while men are beasts. Both "creeds" must be rejected. Cathy Young, author of *Ceasefire: Why Women and Men Must Join Forces to Achieve True Equality* says, ". . . we must accept our differences, underscoring that an armistice in the gender wars is unlikely to work if it focuses on acceptance of collective but not individual differences. She believes that a world divided into updated versions of pink and blue would be only marginally less progressive than a world of khaki uniforms."[21]

In its founders, The Salvation Army was blessed with leaders who were 19th-century futurists in that they anticipated changes far beyond their times. Willing to stand against the cultural norms, Catherine Booth paved the way for women's rights. Evangeline wrote of her mother, "In her protest against all that was half-hearted in the church and iniquitous in the world she was, not less a heroine of the arena, a champion of emancipation."[22]

The Army did not stand alone in its early 19th-century visionary approach. In her book *No Time for*

---

[21] Cathy Young, *Ceasefire! Why Women and Men Must Join Forces to Achieve True Equality,* The Free Press: 1999.
[22] Evangeline Booth, "Woman," pp. 25-26.

Silence, author Janette Hassey documents the vigorous nature of women in ministry during the evangelical resurgence between the Civil War and the rise of fundamentalism in America.

She says there were several factors at work. *The horrible fate of the unsaved,* which motivated believers to ignore social conventions for the good of the lost. *A sense of the nearness of the Second Coming* that predisposed believers to see women's gifts as part of the outpouring of the Spirit. *Social factors.* The social upheaval of the frontier and the desperate needs of the urban areas created an action–oriented atmosphere in which social convention withered and women's ministries blossomed.[23]

In the 20th century, the movement of women toward equality in society was indisputably one of the most significant changes. There is every reason to assume that this movement will continue to make a significant impact far into this new millennium. In their book *Megatrends for Women,* John Naisbitt and Patricia Aburdene point out that while women figure more significantly than ever before in the overwhelming extent of problems worldwide, they also represent a significant force capable of bringing solution to those problems. They say women have pushed themselves beyond the limits that once defined them and have willingly taken over roles that were once the exclusive domain of males—an idea whose time has come, say the authors.[24] This being true, any movement whose mission strategy

---

[23] Janet Hassey, *No Time for Silence,* Zondervan Publishing Company, Academie Books: Grand Rapids, Mich., 1986, p. 123ff.

[24] Patricia Aburdene and John Naisbitt, *Megatrends for Women: Women Are Changing the World,* Arrow Books Limited: London, 1994, xi–xiii.

follows the Puritan plan will be hard-pressed to achieve its objectives.

Roots of Oppression

At the same time, we must understand that oppression of women has deep, stubborn roots in our church and civil traditions. Under Jewish law, for example, a woman was considered to be more a thing than a person. She was at the disposal of her father and husband. Shut out of the synagogue, she had few, if any, religious rights. Her status was that of a slave. Furthermore, thousands of Grecian women were devoted to sacred prostitution and plied their trade on the streets. Respectable women were confined to their homes; only their husbands were allowed to see them. They did not appear at meals; their participation in public meetings was forbidden.

Such deep-rooted oppression did not end in biblical times. In *Women Caught in the Conflict,* Rebecca Merrill Groothuis records that in the 18th century, the English common law of William Blackstone upheld the "civil death" of women who married. She writes, "Blackstone asserted in his *Commentaries,* 'By marriage, the husband and wife are one person in law; that is, the very being or legal existence of the woman is suspended during her marriage, or at least, is consolidated into that of her husband under whose wing, protection and cover she performs everything. Even as he owned his slaves, so a man owned his wife.'"

Groothuis says the issue of women's rights grew out of the fight against slavery. "The first women to become public advocates of abolition were Christians, the ideology of antislavery being equality and independence for all human beings. The cause of abolition provided activist women with an ideology, a methodology and an occasion, which led them formally to organize a campaign for women's rights. This came as a result of their realization that the principle, 'all men are created equal' applied as well to women as it did to slaves."

She continues, "The early feminists' objection to legalised domination of wives by husbands led some couples publicly to renounce such laws upon their marriage." Groothuis points out that before his marriage to Harriet Taylor in 1851, John Stuart Mill wrote a formal protest against the law of marriage, which he said conferred on the husband "legal powers and control over the person, property, and freedom of action of the wife"; he made "'a solemn promise never in any case or under any circumstances' to use such powers.'"

Groothuis also observes, "While their [the Mills'] marriage of mutual love and equality served as an example to others, it served also to highlight the prevailing attitudes of people, both women and men, toward the marriage relationship." She cites one young suitor, himself thoroughly convinced of the iniquity of legalized domination, who wrote, "'I believe nineteen women out of twenty would be unhappy with a husband who, like myself, would repudiate supremacy.'" He goes on to explain that this was "'because the great majority of people, in endeavouring to imagine a contrary state of things, conceive of the woman as the *leader* and the man as the *subservient.*'"

This young suitor promised his fiancé that he would "repudiate the supremacy" of either woman or man in marriage. "'Equality for me is a passion,'" he wrote. "'I dislike equally to assume, or to endure authority.'"And the minister who performed the ceremony for this suitor and his bride commented, "'I never perform the marriage ceremony without a renewed sense of the iniquity of . . . a system by which man and wife are one, and that one is the husband.'"

"Unfortunately," says Groothuis, "this misconception haunts us still. The idea of equality and mutual submission is rarely considered as a possibility. Only two options are recognized: either a man dominates his wife (or female business associate); or his wife (or female business associate) dominates him. Because the idea of a man being dominated by a woman is particularly repugnant to most people, his 'right' to dominate her is retained."[25]

Just how far we've come in repudiating male supremacy within the church is uncertain. How passionate we are in our desire for equality between women and men in ministry is indefinite. I fear the evidence points primarily to apathy. It seems the jury is still out on many of the issues.

Although the number of women duly ordained to ministry with equal rights and privileges of their ordination is growing, the issue of women's ordination has not been fully resolved. The problems of cultural and historical barriers continue to create complex problems that deny women their rightful place and rob both women and men of the solidarity in mission and ministry they desire and deserve.

General Frederick Coutts reminded Salvationists, in

[25] Rebecca Merrill Groothius, *Women Caught in the Conflict: The Culture War Between Traditionalism and Feminism*, Baker Books: Grand Rapids, Mich., 1994, pp. 31–33.

his article written for the *Year Book, 1959,* that "God's ways are not our ways, nor His thoughts our thoughts .... Seeing that the grace of the Spirit and the gift of the office of apostle, prophet, evangelist, pastor and teacher have been and are so undeniably granted to women as well as men 'for the perfecting of the saints, for the work of the ministry, for the edifying of the body of Christ,' who are we to withstand God?"[26]

The call comes to redress in new ways the imbalance of the authority of the masculine and feminine in our lives and in our cultures. Some would argue that a woman should give herself to God and in service to her neighbors, but as Harriet A. Harris of the University of Oxford insists, "We must also ask that woman be able to discover herself so that she has a self to give."

Prevalent among some is a presupposition that because women and men differ physically, their spiritual needs and therefore their responsibilities are also different. *Priscilla Papers,* a journal published by Christians for Biblical Equality (CBE) featured an article by Rebecca Merrill and Douglas Groothuis that makes the point.

> *Biblically, spiritual gifts and qualities do not come in shades of pink and blue! When, for example, the fruit of the Spirit is listed in Galatians 5:22,23, there is not even a hint that some fruit is masculine and some feminine. But just as it is wrong for radical spiritual feminists to insist that there is something spiritually advantageous to being female, so it would be wrong for Christian men to slip into the assumption that maleness is somehow more spiritually important to the cause of Christ—that manliness is next to godliness, as it were ... women and men are both created with the need to love and be loved, to have a sense of life purpose and per-*

[26] Frederick L. Coutts, *The Salvation Army Year Book,* The Salvation Army: London, 1959.

sonal accomplishment, and, ultimately, to glorify God and seek His kingdom (Matt. 6:33, Col. 3:17). Both men and women have these needs, because these are human needs, and men and women are both human.[27]

The biblical truth of the matter, say this husband/wife team, is that there is nothing that Christ did or said . . . that is any less applicable to the life of a godly woman than to the life of a godly man."[28]

Addressing Army Inequalities

Catherine Booth's commitment to biblical equality began within the marriage relationship, in which sub-mission *to one another* becomes the true expression of divine love. And in her view, this same ideal was to be applied to the Christian ministry, enabling women and men equally to respond to the Holy Spirit's call to every kind of service in the Church. What this means is that we are being invited to listen to the voice of God through the lives of women, in both their public and private expression, as well as through the lives of men.

The founders of The Salvation Army fought and won the battles against constitutional restrictions and social conventions that could have impeded women in the Army. If that legacy is to be preserved for subsequent generations, Salvationists today and in the future must take great care to avoid self-imposed or culturally imposed restrictions. As Katherine M. Haubert remarks, "The challenge for the church is to allow the redeeming results of Calvary and Jesus' attitude to shape its views. The church needs to take the sickle of truth and cut

---

[27] Rebecca Merrill and Douglas Groothius, "Women Keep Promises Too! Or The Christian Life Is For Both Men and Women," in *Priscilla Papers,* Spring, 1997, pp. 1-9. See also www.CBEInternational.org.
[28] Ibid.

through the barbed wire of cultural custom and taboo in order to emulate the one who promised both men and women, 'if the Son makes you free, you will be free indeed.'"[29]

Delegates to the International College for Officers in London some years ago listened attentively as Mrs. Commissioner Hilda Cox, now retired, called attention to the fact that "although it is true The Salvation Army holds a very definite view and has a policy of equality between the sexes, it is doing so against a powerful, historical and cultural background concerning attitudes towards women. The misunderstanding of the word 'equality' and its practical outworking still tends to create difficulties."

The good news is that in many parts of the world, the situation is changing. As British novelist Graham Greene has said, "There always comes a moment in time when the door opens and lets the future in." The door of equal opportunity is opening for women in many societies of the world, particularly Western ones, as never before in history. The question is, are we of the people of the Church universal, the people of the evangelical community, indeed, the people of the Army, ready and willing to allow the future in?

Letting in the future is about willing not only the end, but also the means. Over a century ago, Clause 14 of the Foundation Deed of The Christian Mission (three years later to be renamed The Salvation Army) willed the means as it granted to all Salvation Army women officers the right to preach the gospel of Christ and to fulfill the office of clergy. One does observe, however, the wording of the

[29] Katherine M. Haubert, *Women as Leaders: Accepting the Challenge of Scripture,* MARC: Monrovia, Calif., 1993, p. 23.

clause, which states, "Nothing shall authorize the Conference to take any course whereby the right of females ... shall be impeded or destroyed or which shall render females ineligible for any office or ... vote at all or any official meetings *of which they may be members ..."*

Although it is difficult to determine a specific time or place in our history when this occurred, women, particularly married women officers, were effectively barred from strategic boards and councils. This policy not only rendered females ineligible for certain offices; it also inhibited leadership development of married women officers in a variety of ways.

Perhaps those responsible for these policy decisions within the Army followed the pattern of the Church as seen by Dr. Paul K. Jewett:

> *Surely the church as the company of God's people, should manifest its calling to be a redemptive force in the world by striving for full equality in the man/woman relationship ... but through the centuries the church has drawn back, being conformed to this world at one crucial point ... the church has construed the data of revelation through the eyes of the world more than through the eyes of faith; thus limiting the woman's place in ministry. So long as this perspective prevails, the woman will never come into full inheritance. Her place will be that of assistant to the man rather than partner with him. To limit women in ministry when they know they have equal gifts and calling with men, is to threaten their Christian lives with banality.[30]*

At the 1984 International Leaders' Conference in Berlin, Mrs. General Maire Wahlstrom, now retired, appealed to the members to bring Army policy back into line with our heritage. She said, "What can we do in

---

[30] Paul K. Jewett, *The Ordination of Women,* William B. Eerdmans Publishing Company: Grand Rapids, Mich., 1980, pp 100-101.

order to give every woman officer a chance to participate wholeheartedly in the work, an opportunity to feel that she is needed, that she is engaged in meaningful work, that she is able to fulfill her calling, that she is an officer in her own right with all the responsibilities and privileges that go with officership?"

A decade later, General Paul Rader took action in response to recommendations put forward by an international commission established to study issues related to women in ministry. As a result, married women officers were given rank in their own right, including the ranks of lieutenant colonel through commissioner. (The only rank above commissioner is General). This resulted in an unprecedented number of women delegates attending the High Council of 1999. Previously, the High Council was restricted to commissioners and certain other territorial commanders and did not include their spouses, as they did not hold rank in their own right. At the 1999 High Council a married woman commissioner was elected chaplain and for the first time spouses of nominees for General were asked to respond to questions submitted by the council.

There were other changes: Married women officers were permitted to participate on major policy-making boards. This opened the door for spouses of those officers who became members by virtue of their positions on headquarters staff. Furthermore, the spouse of the chairperson was no longer excluded from participation on boards. Those persons serving as territorial presidents of Women's Organizations (traditionally, wives of territorial commanders) became eligible for inclusion as full members of territorial cabinets. Women, married and single, were given greater consideration as possible candidates for conferences, seminars, and other opportunities for personal leadership development. Eventually, the rank of the wife of the General was changed from "Mrs. General" to Commissioner.

Early in his tenure of office, General John Gowans asserted that he welcomed the 28 recommendations of the Commission on Officership "as a means of bringing once again into central focus the powerful notion of flexibility—or, as Catherine Booth would have put it, 'our prime principle of adaptation'—so essential if we are to maintain or, in some cases, regain the cultural relevance and spiritual significance for our own time and place (wherever that may be) which our dauntless forebears had for theirs."[31]

These and other changes significantly enhanced the place and ministry of women in the Army and is enabling them to reach their full potential in the ministry to which they were called, ordained, and commissioned.

Those resistant to change may not view change in a positive light. But change was long overdue. As far back as 1899, a young woman officer engaged to be married wrote to her headquarters officer husband-to-be:"I am practically marrying out of the work. What am I to do? Keep my house nice and once a week visit a hospital? I could have married without becoming an officer and always have been a good soldier, but God called me to be an officer!"

The Army of Tomorrow

Hope springs eternal in the words of General Rader's *Kairos Now* address, presented at the South Asia Zonal Conference, where "activation and empowerment of

---

[31] General John Gowans, taken from *The Officer,* February 2000, pp 11.

women" was stressed emphatically as one of the priorities for mission in the new millennium. He pointed out the underutilized resource available to us in capable women, especially lay Salvationists and married women officers, many of whom have been effectively deactivated, particularly after being appointed to headquarters. Others, General Rader observed, have been afforded only limited opportunities for self-improvement and not a few have been limited by the biases of their own husbands or leaders. It is a shame when secular analysts appear to appreciate the potential contribution of women more than we do, we who are heirs to the New Testament affirmation that both women and men are one in Jesus Christ.

Hope springs eternal in the words of a representative speaker for the great East Africa Territory, the divisional officer of the Thika Yatta Division. In comments directed to the General and me on an Easter Sunday, he said, "We shall remember you for many initiatives, among which are the changes in the role of married women officers, bringing equality with men in rank, respect, opportunity, and consideration." In that moment I knew all would be well for the tens of thousands of East African soldiers and the officers who serve them. Why? Because this male officer leader understands, appreciates, and affirms Catherine's dream.

Hope shines through the testimony of a young Nigerian woman officer as she speaks in officers' councils to her peers, all of whom serve within an area of the world considered by mission strategists of one of the most difficult to evangelize. She says, "I'm not only a preacher, I'm a reacher."

Hope comes alive when I think of the four young

girls we met in Uganda and thousands of others; I am encouraged by young, enthusiastic, well-educated women who stand tall among members of Parliament, or similar positions as representatives of their government. Among those we were privileged to meet in the East Africa Territory was a young Ugandan woman who, with her daughter, Patricia, attended the Congress Sunday morning meeting. "When someone asks me which of my two children I would educate if I had money only for one," she confided, "I tell them my daughter, Patricia. My son would manage on his own, but without education, there is no hope for my daughter."

This Ugandan woman named Hope lives to spread hope among the poor. She works hard providing Uganda's women with segments of land where they grow crops, sell produce, earn enough to take care of themselves and their families. A small amount to be sure, yet highly significant in the lives of Uganda's poor. Against all odds, the women have also earned a reputation for 100 percent payback on their loans.

These and other forms of micro-enterprise are catching on in many parts of the world. In a number of countries women are discovering how to address societal problems in innovative, although at times culturally unconventional ways.

Increasingly, the culture of silence is being broken— with love, care, and understanding—on issues such as physical abuse, rape, family, and community conflict. Salvationist women, in concert with women clergy and lay leaders of other denominations, are discovering that being encumbered by traditions from another era may indeed become "the encumbrance, and the sin which so easily entangles us" (Hebrews 12:1, *NASV*), creating barriers to effective leadership and mission can be frustrating. Women in ministry, both lay and clergy, are eager to join hands and hearts to accomplish God's purposes because theirs is a shared vision. But the partnership they desire is an authentic partnership, one that is based on what they can contribute.

These women envision a Church that leads the world on issues of social justice, a Church that accepts women and men as equals and helps them live integrated lives, a Church that helps women fulfill their responsibilities and contribute to all aspects of mission and ministry. They envision searching for ways they can contribute to the whole body of Christ.

If this vision is to be fully realized, the Church must be willing to own its decisions regarding the woman's role. The Army is no exception. Women must accept the challenge and seize opportunities for making full proof of their ministry. Catherine fought the battles using the weaponry available in 19th-century England. However, in the week she died, she issued a solemn warning that she feared the women of The Salvation Army were not going to rise up to take the place she wished for them.

We've come a long way regarding women's rights in the workplace. We've come a long way regarding women's rights in ministry. But the fact remains, for every glass ceiling in the corporate world, there is a stained-glass ceiling in the Church. We must never allow women of the Army to be "ceilinged." We must never lose sight of Catherine's ideals. She believed Christ's principle was to put woman on the same platform as man; her dream must be kept alive.

The message of the Army regarding women's role is not about woman power or man power. It is not about a radical, secular, arrogant, derogatory feminism. This is about deploying our people full force to win a sin–darkened 21st–century world to Jesus Christ. It is about women and men becoming true partners in mission in order to evangelize effectively. It is about partnership in the great and privileged task of accomplishing the Great Commission during our lifetime. It is about the attitude of Jesus, who commissioned women to be the first heralds of the glorious good news of the Resurrection. It is about following the example of our Lord Jesus, who believed in the worth and validity of women so much that it is said of Him that He companioned women to dignity and ministry. It is about the emancipation proclamation of the apostle Paul, who declared, "There is no such thing as Jew and Greek, slave and freeman, male and female; for you are all one person in Christ Jesus ..." (Gal. 3:28, *NEB*).

It is about keeping alive the dream of the founders, William and Catherine Booth. We have come a long way in recent years, but there is a road ahead, and we must keep it an open road, a road to the future for women and men, married and single. It's about keeping the Army, the Army.

In 1914, two years after the founder was promoted to Glory, Mrs. Commissioner George Scott Railton [Marianne], wrote a tribute to William Booth for *The War Cry*. The article was entitled, "Our Path Finder— Women's Thanksgiving for the Life and Work of General William Booth." She writes:

> *"We claim for our late beloved General that he found the long–closed road by which women might carry out their Lord's command. Ah, but he saw that the path must be made wide and straight and unmistakable, or it would close again! He made very straight paths for our feet. He believed in our*

fitness and by giving us the opportunity, he proved it to the world. His legacy to us is our absolute freedom to preach, to organize and to carry on the work of Christ's Kingdom on an equality with men in our Army of Salvation. He has found us a path. Let us see to it that the road so opened is worthily trodden and never again allowed to be closed.[32]

"The Lord gave the command, and many women carried the news" (Psalm 68:11, *Good News Bible*).

---

[32] Marianne Railton, "Our Path Finder—Women's Thanksgiving for the Life and Work of General William Booth," in *The War Cry,* August 22, 1914, p. 7.

❧ BIBLIOGRAPHY ❧

Aburdene, Patricia and Naisbitt, John. *Megatrends for Women: Women Are Changing the World.* London: Arrow Books Limited, 1994.

Adamson, Peter. "A Failure in Imagination," in *The Progress of Nations.* New York: UNICEF House, 1996.

Bolt, Robert. *A Man For All Seasons.* New York: Random House, Inc., 1962.

Booth, Evangeline. *Woman.* New York: Fleming H. Revell Company, 1930.

Booth, William. "Wesleyan Conference Address," *The War Cry.* London: The Salvation Army.

Bunch, Charlotte. "Women Suffer the World Over," *The War Cry* of the United Kingdom Territory, 118th year, No. 6314.

Coutts, Frederick L. *The Salvation Army Year Book.* London: The Salvation Army, 1959.

Groothuis, Rebecca Merrill. *Women Caught in the Conflict: The Culture War Between Traditionalism and Feminism.* Grand Rapids, Mich.: Baker Books, 1994.

Hassey, Janet. *No Time for Silence.* Grand Rapids, Mich.: Zondervan Publishing Company, 1986.

Haubert, Katherine M. *Women as Leaders: Accepting the Challenge of Scripture.* Monrovia, Calif.: MARC, 1993.

Jewett, Paul K. *The Ordination of Women.* Grand Rapids, Mich.: William B. Eerdmans Publishing Company, 1980.

Kroeger, Richard Clark and Catherine Clark. *I Suffer Not a Woman: Rethinking I Timothy 2:11-15 in Light of Ancient Evidence.* Grand Rapids, Mich.: Baker Book House, 1992.

Montgomery, Laura. "Girls as Goods: The Problem of Child Prostitution," in *Together, a Journal of World Vision International,* January–March 1996.

Parkin, Christine. "A Woman's Place," in Kew, Clifford, ed., *Catherine Booth, Her Continuing Relevance.* St. Albans, Vt.: The Campfield Press, 1990.

Purves, Libby. *More Lives Than One.* London: Hodder and Stoughton Publishing Company, 1998.

Toubia, Nabial. "Sources, FGM," in *The Progress of Nations,* New York: UNICEF House, 1996.

Yancey, Philip. *The Jesus I Never Knew.* Grand Rapids, Mich.: Zondervan Publishing House, 1995.